Essays in Economics

Savio Gomes

Essays in Economics

Savio Gomes

Publishing
Paving Ways For New Writers

First Published in 2018 by First Step Publishing
Editorial / Sales / Marketing Office at
303-304 Garnet Nirmal Lifestyles Ph 2
Behind Nirmal Lifestyles Mall
LBS Marg Mulund West
Mumbai 400080
E-Mail:- info@firststepcorp.com
www.firststepcorp.com

ISBN:- 978-93-83306-44-2
Cover Designed by: Design Fishing
Price: INR 650 in India Rest $10

Contents

Dedicated to

My Mother Remy Gomes

Introduction

Essays in Economics includes a series of essays written in the years 2010 – 2012. The focus is not on pure economic theory but on the practice of economics from macroeconomic and a behavioral perspectives. The essays have been set up in this book merely in alphabetical order of their titles.

Economic development, contrary to most political and theoretical premises, is based on individual choices. It is the small and medium entrepreneur, the ancillaries and households that are usually the better leading economic indicators.

Income inequality is here to stay and is probably a good stimulus of economic activity. Unequal distribution of wealth creates and fuels aspiration which is the basic engine of economic activity

Global warming and environmental issues are real costs on all continents. Global warming when treated with religious fervor rather than practical utility has few positives.

Food security is a problem of logistics as one way or the other the world actually has enough resources.

Humans are not efficient at recycling waste and will probably never do so economically on a large scale.

Social media is a disruptive force which has yet to prove its merits either socially, politically or economically.

Education needs to shift to useful technical and job related skills. The focus today is too much on knowledge that is not regularly applied in life or business situations. AI does not threaten talent or skills. AI threatens knowledge databases that are relational. Social skills, networking, communication and presentation outweigh knowledge based skills. Public libraries and reading should be encouraged. The human mind has a sharper learning curve than any AI system.

Political parties are best run as corporate for purposes of transparency of motive and fund raising. Corruption in free running politics, unregulated and their sources of funds is a key contributory factor in deviant governance. Religious entities, NGOs, charitable institutions and agricultural holdings above a minimum size ought to be taxable based on collections. Wealth held and/ or controlled by these exceeds the organized industrial and services sector in many instances. If these are not to be taxed directly then the entire economy should only be taxed indirectly through expenditure taxes.

Prison systems need to be effectively replaced, except in the worst criminal cases by social reform and community service programs. Prison sentences are a huge economic and social loss. As is compulsory military service.

Price discrimination across regions, customer groups, timing of service and minor product variants, is essential to stimulating market development and innovation. Price discrimination when regulated constricts growth. Indiscriminate price discrimination is in fact an indicator of a healthy free market.

Interest rates should be maintained steady over reasonably long periods by central banks. Open market operations and taxation are better fiscal and monetary tools than variations in interest rates.
Credit for individuals and businesses should be limited to six month's sustainable income. Graduating to this norm would eliminate bubbles in the financial and real estate markets as well as reduce non-performing assets of banks.

Inflation should be controlled through consumer unions in each sector deciding what prices may be paid reasonably for each half year. Inflation decisions by producers or bankers is immoral and antisocial. Inflation expectations on the grounds of a wage rise and reduction in taxes is often without foundation since there may or may not be a demand-supply gap or a cost push.

Economic sanctions are a fool's political tool and provide no real benefit whilst hurting all around. Economic sanctions hurt the sanctioned and the 'sanctioner'.

Public spending and the role of government should be minimized to defense, education, infrastructure and the like. Expenditure on defense itself is counter-productive. Japan and Germany for instance grew into industrial strong men after WW2 only on account of their virtually non-existent defense spending. Defense wastes resources like no other sector.

Cash based and barter economies are efficient, and generally more reliable than banking systems. Even on a country wide basis, the cash run section of the economy is clearly more efficient and grows at a faster pace providing more employment opportunities.

Free trade is a blunder since subsidies and tariffs exist in every country under one guise or the other.

Pension schemes in fact like insurance, serve no economic good and should be gradually unwound and liquidated. Pension schemes are a social evil which erode savings and economic stimulus whilst placing a burden on future generations.

Economic indicators such as GDP, inflation, consumer prices are usually inaccurate and misleading, in all economies, more so in controlled economies such as China. The only real indicator of economic development is the index of the cost of a haircut. Read on and hopefully enjoy.

2100

It is the time of the year when people who believe in the Mayan hypothesis expect the world to come to a sort of halt around its axis this December. For those who do not believe, here are some things likely to change by the year 2100. Mandarin is currently spoken by around 14 percent of the world's population, Hindi nearly 5 percent, English just over 5 percent and Arabic by a little over 4 percent. By the year 2100, Mandarin will be spoken by over 25 percent, Hindi by around 20 percent (on an average, randomly anywhere around the world, one in three individuals at any service queue, will speak Mandarin or Hindi) and English by only around 4 percent of the world's population. The shift in the landscape of the spoken language has important ramifications for the education sector and for global companies. The odds are most certainly in favour of call centre agents in Spain, Greece, Italy, Australia, and Portugal taking calls in Mandarin, Hindi and Arabic by 2100.

The health landscape favours those who have stayed away from steroids and chemical concoctions. A leading health magazine recently presented the top 20 fittest men of modern time. Among the top athletes on the list are Michael Phelps, Bruce Lee and Jack LaLanne. Jack who was an American fitness and nutritional expert, passed away in 2011 at the age of 96. LaLanne advocated the benefits of regular exercise and a healthy diet. LaLanne who was variously called the godfather of fitness, and the first fitness superhero, at the age of 54 came out ahead of a 21 year old Schwarzenegger in an informal contest, and later served on Governor Schwarzenegger's council of physical fitness. The market for men's 'health' supplements and steroids is over a billion dollars annually in the USA alone, almost forty percent of which is use (or abuse) by adolescents. Herschel Walker, Jim Thorpe and Muhammad Ali are the other notable athletes on the list. The case for the health supplements industry is simply unsupported by empirical evidence over the last hundred years. This is one industry that is not predicted to be around 50 years from now.

While steroids are mostly bad news for health, asteroids are great news for the minerals and metals industry. A single asteroid of around two kilometres in diameter has a mass of thirty billion tones. Such an asteroid could contain 500 times the earth's reserves of platinum, 4,000 times the reserves of cobalt, and at least 20 times our reserves of metals such as iron and nickel. The US based Planetary Resources (backed by such luminaries as Larry Page, Eric Schmidt and Simonyl of Google and Microsoft) is focused on scanning near earth objects to understand their potential for mining. Most key elements (cobalt, copper, zinc, gold, lead, tin, and silver for example) that support modern industry are likely to run out by 2100. Along with English no longer being the global language of commerce by 2100, science is likely to have to invent whole new systems of technology that are no longer dependent on traditional metals. Television sets, music systems, and batteries are going to have to look very different later this century since their basic components and power systems will be entirely new. Either that or there will be underground mining on near earth asteroids (Lord of the Rings' middle earth?).

Air New Zealand's new in flight safety video includes hobbits, and elves who strap themselves in, take a look at life vests and safety exits. There is even a Gandalf in the pilot's seat and the tagline is Airline of Middle Earth. The hobbit inspired video supported by a clever script and jokes has been viewed nearly three million times on YouTube.

A Fine Web

Sweden is best at using the Web according to recent report by Tim Berners-Lee. His Web Index ranked 61 countries on the basis of Web use, content, impact of the internet and infrastructure. The study included five years data and a year of surveys. Google funded the report with a $ 1 million grant. The USA came in second and was ranked no.1 in terms of access to Web content. Iceland topped in terms of internet infrastructure and utilization of the Web, over 95 percent of Icelanders use the internet. Singapore was mentioned as having fastest internet speeds, whereas Ireland's economy benefited the most from the internet (Ireland's communication related exports amount to around 15% of its GDP). Developing countries did not fare well, for example, only one in six Africans have access to the internet, and the last ranked on the list included Zimbabwe, Burkina Faso in Africa and Yemen. Apparently, social media notwithstanding, knowledge and participation in today's society and economy, is still a costly affair.

Pfizer the pharmaceutical giant was recently fined $ 60 million by regulatory authorities in the USA for bribing doctors and government officials in various countries (Asia, Middle East and Eastern Europe). In an effort to boost sales, Pfizer was held guilty of paying out millions of dollars in bribes to officials in Bulgaria, Kazakhstan, Russia and other countries. Among the mechanisms used by Pfizer to boost sales were exclusive distributorship agreements, cash payments to prescribers, fees for 'motivation of officials', 'honorariums', and 'hospital programs' designed to motivate prescriptions. Other drug companies held guilty and fined for dubious marketing practices include GlaxoSmithKline ($3 billion in settlements), Teva of Israel (allegations of bribery in Latin American countries), and Johnson & Johnson. Johnson & Johnson (J&J) agreed to a $181 million settlement for improper marketing practices related to a drug, including misleading patients and doctors about associated risks.

The extraction of misleading practices continues in harsh economic times. Peter Cummings, the former head of corporate lending at HBOS was recently hauled up by the Financial Services Authority (FSA) in the UK. Cummings has been fined 500,000 sterling pounds, and has been banned for life from working in financial services. Cummings was blamed for leading a 'culture of optimism', aggressive expansion strategy and ignoring known risks. Aggressive lending practices resulted in huge losses at HBOS. Cumming's policies, in part, led to a spurt in commercial property loans from 2006 to 2008 (around 68 billion sterling pounds at HBOS). Cummings has it appears, resented that he is the only individual from HBOS to face such censure and stated that other senior people were also involved in the process. At the other end of the spectrum of defaulters and banking fiascos, we have social banking. The world's first social investment bank Big Society Capital (BSC) is likely to make investments up to 37 million sterling pounds, linked to socially desirable outcomes. Payments on the basis of social results are

17

on the upswing and investors will be able to participate in funds that will invest in specific social outcomes. The Boston Consulting Group's report stated that the demand in the social investment market in the UK would reach one billion sterling pounds by 2016. BSC will also invest in The Results Fund (finance for payment by results government contracts) and Impact Ventures UK Fund (growth capital for socially motivated enterprises).

The Rebel Entrepreneur is a book by Jonathan Moules. Moules advises budding entrepreneurs not to get hung up on business plans and to accept failure as part of the learning curve. Moules advises new businesses not to use venture capital funding, and to use imaginative methods to resolve crises and errors. His business rules, however, are more designed for technologically disruptive, evolutionary and rebellious businesses.

Acca Dacca

The official song for businesses emerging out of the recession appears to be the AC/ DC (in Australia – 'Acca Dacca') album 'Back in Black'. The album has sold an estimated 49 million units worldwide, including around 20 million units in the USA alone. A note of caution, however, from Matt Waller, (a tour operator in Southern Australia), is that this also appears to be the top favourite album of great white sharks and, playing 'Back in Black' while at the ocean, is not advised, unless the objective is to click rows of serrated teeth.

Steel represents over 95 percent of all metals used each year. The end of a 40 year benchmark system and, the sharp rise in the market price of iron ore has led to big gains for iron ore producers. The next person likely to attain the tag of the richest individual in the world is Australian Gina Rinehart, who has developed her family business into a massive portfolio of iron ore and coal production operations. Given the immensely sooty and profitable nature of the business, it is a more than appropriate case for a rendition of 'Back in Black'. Interestingly, the band Acca Dacca was considered a pioneer of heavy metal.

Meanwhile, the world continues to grow increasingly flat. The flatbread *tandoor* oven dates back to around 2,600 B.C. in India and, the core of *tandoori* cooking has its origins in India's northwest frontier. The *tandoor* was a personal favourite of the emperor Shah Jahan who also gave the world the Taj Mahal. The world's most famous *tandoor* producer is astonishingly – not an Indian, but an American – Ron Levy, a former ceramic artist is the creator of designer *tandoors*. Levy's 'Home-door' *tandoors* are made in Ohio. New Call Telecom is another example of the shifting sands of global trade and economics. The British company carried out a cost and service analysis study and discovered that after taking into account labour and rental costs, it was more cost effective to locate their work centre in Lancashire, than in India. Outsourcing to India is no longer necessarily a cheaper alternative.

The piece of real estate most likely to witness sky rocketing prices over the next ten months is not located in Asia, the USA or in the UK. Xul (pronounced Shool) is at Yucatan, Mexico. It is a few miles from where the world nearly ended 65 million years ago, ground zero for the Chicxulub asteroid that wiped out our friends Dino and cousins. The lush green hillsides have attracted wealthy individuals to build bunker like buildings in preparation for the next Armageddon, anticipated in December 2012, at the end of the Mayan calendar.

The Self-Storage sector in the US has experienced sharp growth in the past couple of years. Self-storage businesses provide secure lockers, rooms, containers, 24 hour access, climate controlled, and outdoor storage space for personal effects and equipment. Nearly 58,000 storage facilities in the US cater to around 45 million Americans forced to move each year. Self-storage auctions of sealed lots, which have fallen behind in rental payments, are also a feverish favourite with some.

At the other end of the Pacific, the Japanese are having a hard time of the global recession. Japanese housewives track family spending and run household budgets, using a budget book called the 'kakeibo'. An allowance is doled out each month to their 'salarymen' husbands. Salarymen's allowances have hit a 29 year low at around US$ 450 a month and, wives' secret savings (hesokuri) dropped by over 15 percent in 2010. One impact of the dwindling discretionary male and female pocket purses is that Japan's high divorce rate (over 27%) has begun dropping.

Affluenza

It is widely recognized now that the global threat of the 21st century is not the terror of an influenza virus, rather the errors of the Affluenza virus, afflicting developed nations. The Affluenza virus is characterized by an intense need to buy, grow, buy, borrow and borrow more. The virtuous G5, G7 nations are now followed by the GASP default nations (Greece, America, Spain and Portugal). The eternal spy Mr. Bond is likely to be familiar to future generations as '007 – licensed to bankrupt' and will probably introduce himself as 'Bond – Junk Bond'.

A gross national product that does not measure the quality of health care, education, public integrity, intellectual capital (in fact all that is of real importance to people) has diminished value in this new age. The change in investment climate is real, in many ways more real than geophysical climate change.

The new age assets are databases, processes, knowledge, education content, brands etc. Assets are real only if they facilitate the abilities to compete, communicate and collaborate. Innovation is no longer a crutch to mass production; it is a core business purpose. The age of albedo personalities and mega business organizations that dwell in virtual echo chambers, listen to themselves, and reflect symmetrically consistent ideas and structures, is all but over. Change is the norm and is no longer a US presidential campaign fad.

Capitalists, however, now profess to have discovered the life raft of a solution that promises to restore a semblance of stability to the business ecosystem. A capitalist solution that has emerged from the clouded waters of communal socialism. In 1995, an American trained economist Mohammed Yunus (now Nobel Laureate) first used the term 'socially conscious capitalist enterprise'. Richard DeVos (two heart by pass operations and a later heart transplant recipient), wrote in 1993 about Compassionate Capitalism. Jed Emerson's 'Blended Value Enterprise' focuses on a multiple layered bottom line, which includes economic, social and environmental values generated by a business unit.

The Grameen Bank, Grameen Intel and Grameen Danone are off shoots. These *social business enterprises* (in the USA, Container Store and Whole Foods are examples) are founded on the principle that sustainable profitability is a result of balancing needs of all stakeholders. The socially conscious capitalist enterprise is a co-operative partnership between all stakeholders, customers and employees being the core constituents. The Grameen Bank set new benchmarks in rates of loan repayment, savings and low levels of business failure. These 'Firms of Endearment' have a business purpose that is more than just generating profits.

In a strange new world, rising interest rates in India and China are leading to a preference for zero coupon bonds. A proposed carbon tax in Australia could cause the loss of 14,000 jobs and over USD 20 billion of coal exports, while actually worsening greenhouse gas emissions as the demand for Australian coal is replaced by coal mined from more emission intensive coal producing areas in other countries – a proposed solution? Culling of the camel population in Australia to slow global warming instead of the carbon tax !

In a stranger new world, an apple a day no longer keeps the doctor away. The Environmental Working Group in the US, recently published a report that the apple is the food product most contaminated by pesticides. 92% of apples tested contained two or more pesticides that were used mainly to increase shelf life. And the ubiquitous business card (dating back to 15th century China and 17th century Europe) is now being replaced by Twitter handles, smart cards with Quick Response codes and contact sharing/networking sites such as linked in.com, hashable.com, about me and applications such as Card Munch – *all new symbols of Affluenza.*

All Work and No Play

A German 11 year old boy was in the news recently, for dialling the emergency number 110 to complain about being made to do forced labour (he was asked to tidy up at home after playing). Germany's success as a manufacturing base is however, largely due to its practical education system. Germany's gymnasiums are places of intellectual education. Schooling and apprenticeship are combined and provides children from age 11, with options of training in one or more of 350 trades. Students spend time in classrooms and on factory shop floors. Polish Gimnazjums are for students from the ages of 13 to 16. There are also evening gymnasiums for adults and working students above the age of 14. No wonder that a lot of jobs in the EU go to better trained and skilled labour from Germany and Poland.

All work and no play will make Jack a dull boy' is an old saying. All play and no funding, however, will make sport an unsustainable play. Golf is one sport that does not face the funding issues that the NBA, NFL or Spanish football players (many of whom have not been paid for months), are grappling with. Part of the reason is the unique commercial structure of golf as a sport. Golf in the USA is a good example of social responsibility and good common sense. All PGA Tour events are encouraged to incorporate as charities. Net proceeds are returned to the local communities that host the events. People who work to run each tournament are mostly volunteers. Corporate sponsorships are also easier to come by as a result of the charitable objects. Television accounts for a significant portion of the game's revenues because of unique deals involving upfront payment by sponsors of advertising time. The PGA Tour has exciting plans to open hundreds of retail shops in China and golf will be a sport at the Olympics in Brazil. Charity begins at home and profits begin in China.

Venezuela has announced plans to physically transfer all its overseas gold (most of it in London), back to the country. Only a small fraction of gold is actually moved physically around the world and Venezuela's plans to relocate over 200 tonnes of gold is perhaps the largest ever planned physical move of gold. With so much gold on the move, there are probably newer versions of 'Bank Job' and 'Pirates of the Caribbean' in the making.

A *dabbawallah* strike takes place once in 120 years. The famed *dabbawallahs* who supply mid-day meals to hundreds of thousands of white collar office workers in Mumbai, India have observed a one day strike, their first ever, in support of an anti-corruption crusade. Weather and calamities have not previously stopped the *dabbawallahs* from operating, an operation that has been the study of top management schools in the USA, for its outstanding precision and consistency despite using low end technology and systems. What is truly amazing is that, this hyper efficient delivery system had some serious difficulties in organizing a strike – nobody in the system knew how to stop work.

'Don't let them take your freedom' is the latest song of the German band Gnadenkapelle. The song is not about oppressed people or in fact about any people. It advocates the cause of Yvonne, a six year old freedom loving cow that escaped from its farm in Bavaria, abandoning her sister Waltraud, son Friesi, and prospective suitor Ernst. Yvonne has a Facebook page with over 23,000 'likes' and a Euro 10,000 reward awaits people who help locate her. In Bavaria, commercial farmers take their cows seriously and, just maybe, Bavarian cows too have access to mobile phones and social media.

Angry After 8s

The world economies and financial markets (developed and developing alike) are agitated and angry (annualized gross realized yields) have fallen rather steeply recently. To the embarrassment of western TV channels, news coverage showed only minor differences between the streets of Mogadishu and London. The wild irony of the global financial markets is that debtor nations have AAA rating, whereas their creditor nations have much lower credit ratings – and nobody really knows why the debtors are rated higher than the creditors. 'After 8s', used to represent a brand of classic thin mint dark chocolate. In the UK, 'After 8s' now represents economically disadvantaged groups who roam the streets, making the streets unsafe. In major western cities, life after 8 on the streets is a world apart from life during working hours for people with jobs.

The business and economic environments are in the process of becoming seriously inverted. The 17 countries with AAA ratings include some of the biggest borrowers, with high unemployment and huge inequalities in distribution of income – unemployed roam the streets at night, looking for 'fun' and opportunities to lay waste to life and property. A major bank in New York has been reported to be considering charging fees on cash deposits – cash deposits above a specified amount will not earn, rather they will be charged a fee. This is because the transient, shifting nature of large cash transfers, from other investment classes, makes it difficult for the bank to manage costs of deposit insurance and costs of maintaining regulatory deposit ratios. Banks in India, at the other end of the spectrum, are in the process of taking away the minimum balance requirement charges as account holders invest across the board in local debt instruments, mutual funds and equities. As if these inversions were not enough, Michelin (famous, star awarding, food guides and culinary bible) has a new gastronome director – who currently heads marketing for a motorcycle tyres division.

Business, politics and media are completely intertwined in the USA and UK. The News Corps' recent trials are evidence. MF Global Holdings ('MF') in the USA astonished even the most hardened cynics in an almost unambiguous admission of the rich and deep government - business nexus. MF reportedly structured a US$ 300 million bond issue with a one percent higher interest rate if its CEO resigned - to join the administration as Treasury Secretary or White House economic advisor or other top Federal post. MF's CEO just happens to be a large fund raiser for the 2012 Presidential re-election campaign. The implications of this declaration of interest (conflict of) are simply mind boggling. Close on the appointment of a French politician with no background in economics, as head of the IMF, this is another sign of key economic appointments in developed economies being made on the basis of partisan political considerations, rather than sound common sense. It also underlines the unhealthy nexus between the political systems and economic policies – a key reason why the After 8s are so unhappy with the difficulties of 'un- governance' that they are confronted with.

We may yet see hauling coals to Newcastle as a practical possibility and not a classic business contrarian spoof. One of the largest producers (and exporters) of chopsticks is in Americus city, Georgia State - USA. Georgia Chopsticks operates 24/7 and exports millions of pieces every day to China. One of the very few 'Made in the USA' daily use products sold in China, Japan and Korea. The company is owned by a Korean – American. The chopsticks are disposable and therefore, the business is likely to be around for a long time. China is probably working overtime on an 'anti - dumpling' duty policy.

A-noying

'Noynoy' used to be a person's name, then a noun and now a verb. The President of the Philippines is popularly known as 'Noynoy'. Noynoy was elected in 2010 with impeccable credentials. His critics alleging inaction have designed a unique protest gimmick. 'Noynoying' includes people standing or lying down or resting their heads and staring vacantly around. Gandhi would have appreciated this tongue in cheek form of non-violent protest. Of course, in some countries, with the level of work ethics, nobody would notice the difference. The President, however, enjoys a high approval rating of over 70 percent, implying that in times of financial crisis, no action may actually be seen as a reasonably good course of action.

Sweden holds the distinction of being the first European country to introduce currency notes in 1661. In most Swedish cities today, cash is not 'fash-ion'. Small businesses, public buses, even some places of religious worship do not accept cash, while a number of bank branches do not process cash. Notes and coins represent less than 3 percent of Sweden's economy. Some striking benefits are that the shift to card or phone payments makes theft and corruption much harder. However, bank charges do add up and the anonymity of the person making the payment cannot be retained. Rural communities and the elderly are also likely to be put off by the reliance on non-cash based payment systems (NCPs). NCPs are seen as a convenience or annoying feature in a developed economy. However, in developing countries access to a mobile phone payment system is often easier than access to a bank branch. Meanwhile, the Bank of France will book a profit of nearly 500 million Euros thanks to citizens who hoarded the franc and did not swap them for Euros. The French franc was effectively discontinued recently, and the currency created for Jean "le Bon" in 1360 (as his ransom after a defeat) is no longer legal tender.

Brazil's gross domestic product grew by less than 3 percent in 2011. The problems of the EU (Brazil's key trading partner), have directly and immediately impacted the economy. Brazil, however, is now the world's sixth largest economy, ahead of the UK. The government continues to struggle with balancing inflation, lending rates, growth rates, pension reform, reducing levels of corruption, rationalizing the tax regime and government spending. The sharp rise in the currency has also damaged commodity and manufacturing exports. Government spending flows mainly into state payrolls and this limits the capacity to fund developments in infrastructure, education and health. The cost of doing business ('Custo Brasil') in Brazil is high, taxation and labour welfare policies do not help. The cost of not doing business in Brazil, however, could be much higher for global players.

Governments, investors and the general public have a love, hate and, regulate relationship with parking lots and taxi cabs. Drivers of London's black cabs need to pass tests that can take up to four years to complete, and make the finance certification courses look easy. Some cities have strict operating geographical limits for taxi licenses (e.g. Rome and Mumbai), whereas most cities regulate fares. Other cities restrict operating times, regulate vehicle emission norms, regulate type of fuel used and shared taxi or private taxi operators. Low or no regulation could mean too many taxi cabs on the road, higher traffic congestion, more city pollution and absence of a transparent fare structure. A cab driver who had purchased a NY taxi medallion in the early 1980's for less than $100,000 could auction it today for over $700,000 or alternatively, collect a rent of around $50,000 a year. Horse drawn carriages or bullock carts never did present such challenging dynamics, except for the little annoying issue of cleaning up the roads after.

Bank On It

The 335 page report released recently, by the Senate's Permanent Subcommittee on Investigations harshly condemned HSBC. The bank, in the United States was used as an illicit gateway into the financial system. Mexican drug lords, Iran, terrorist groups, North Korea – all benefitted from lack of adequate compliance. Billions of dollars in cash were transported for drug lords, by the banks' bulk money transfer business. UK's financial regulators fined HSBC over $16 million for selling products inappropriately to vulnerable elderly customers.

Elsewhere, Barclays is being hauled up for attempting to set the 'Liebor'. The British Banker's Association developed the LIBOR, as an average of daily estimates of participating banks. The LIBOR now serves as the benchmark rate for nearly $400 trillion of financial contracts, loans, credit card dues and mortgages. The rate setting process always included 'trimmed averages' (excluding the top and lower end estimates). What was not so well recognized is that the participating banks, in addition, performed their own trimming. Mr. Diamond of Barclays made a quick and inglorious exit, having previously made headlines for his defence of banker's bonuses. Since he took over as CEO, the share prices of Barclays underperformed UK banks by 14 percent and US banks by nearly 25 percent.

Diamonds it appears are not forever, at least not any longer. The phrase 'you can bank on it' has also found its way to the trash heap, along with the valuation basis of a 'risk free rate'. Nobody can bank on a bank anymore. Lesser known banking escapades include David Firth, a Barclays banker in Hampshire, who was sentenced to over seven years in prison for dealing cocaine at this desk (probably trying to recoup a lower bonus?). In another high profile case, Trevor Collenette a retired Lloyds banker was caught out with nearly $12 million worth of cocaine aboard a yacht he was crewing.

Mark Zuckerberg has given a whole new dimension and meaning to the term 'the 1%'. Zuckerberg was able to refinance the mortgage on his Palo Alto home with a 30 year adjustable rate loan starting at 1.05%. The long term borrowing costs available to high net worth individuals in the US are close to 1%. 'The 1%' phrase popularized by the Occupy Wall Street movement, emphasizes that financial systems in the US are designed to perpetuate severe income inequalities. 30 year mortgages in the US for the 99 percent, now average 3.7 percent.

Cities in the USA, are planning to use 'eminent domain' to acquire mortgages for homes that are underwater (current values are less than the mortgages). Eminent domain is usually invoked for the acquisition of private lands for roads, airports and other public use. Fontana CA, San Bernardino County and Ontario CA, are at the forefront of the controversial exercise of eminent domain. Steven Gluckstern, of Mortgage Resolution Partners laid a unique proposal before San Bernardino County. He proposed that the County use 'eminent domain' to seize underwater mortgages, and replace these with mortgages that reflect current market values, with reduced monthly payments. The Californian rebels do not trust the financial donors on Wall Street, especially in an election year. The seizure of mortgages and forced reductions was seen as the only solution, in a scenario where masses of foreclosures shut down whole communities. Meanwhile, Wall Street donors continue to fund presidential campaigns, probably trying to pay off the mortgage on the White House. In the US, over $580 billion of mortgages are underwater, involving over2 million homes.

In an unguarded spell of bald realism, India's central bank governor compared higher borrowing costs for lower income groups, with the rising costs of his haircuts and the inversely thinning of his ageing hairline. The central bank governor's barber clearly believes that reducing rates will not stimulate growth.

Blocked Bloc

'A state of civil strife on account of the immense burden of their debt', 'the majority of creditors made voluntary concessions', 'arranged for the repayment in 10 annual instalments' - these are not phrases from recent proceedings in the EU – these are from historical records around 173BC from regions of Roman era that are now better known in modern times as Greece. History does repeat itself, many times over. . The advocates of the Euro failed to learn the lessons of the disintegration of the USSR in 1990-91.

Maastricht is an old European city that bears the somewhat dubious distinction of being the birthplace of the Euro. The residents of Maastricht have moved from supporters, to disenchanted supporters, to cynics to plain antagonists of the Euro. A common currency bloc, in retrospect seems as absurd as having a common dress code, common diet, common housing arrangements or even a common tax structure. The disintegration of the EU in turn, now seems only a matter of time, while political manoeuvring attempts to provide the financial system with a soft landing. Whereas a global currency such as the US dollar is a necessity, a common bloc currency is a proven (twice over with the Russians and the Europeans) recipe for all round economic disaster. Mr. Obama and Mr. Cameron promised change, their voters, unilaterally, assumed that the change would be for the better and wrote that into their promise.

It was only recently and after over 20 years of dedicated research, that it was discovered that the folds on the neckline of Mona Lisa's dress contained the answer to a long standing mathematical puzzle. Leonardo Da Vinci squared the circle – creating a circle and square of exactly equal area, in around 1505. High definition photographs of the masterpiece revealed an interlocking octagonal pattern (not typical of garment designs of the period) that appeared as embroidered knots along the neckline. Leonardo Da Vinci worked on the Mona Lisa for nearly 16 years and historians are yet to uncover all the secrets of the painting. Mona Lisa and Da Vinci both smile at scholars who have spent decades, tied in knots, attempting to uncover the underlying mathematical solutions painted into the portrait. Europeans are probably hoping that the painting also contains hidden financial secrets.

Empirical research has shown that the solution to managing health care is not costlier insurance or even broader coverage. The solution lies in incentivizing people to look after their own health. In a programme in South Africa, individuals earn points for exercising and eating healthy leading to rewards such as reduced insurance premiums. The programme's alliances with grocery chains and airlines offers discounts based on points earned by making healthy lifestyle choices. Similarly, devices installed in cars can monitor aggressive driving, sharp acceleration and sharp swings. Car owners can earn points for safe driving that link up with discounts on car insurance and even on car maintenance costs. Some of these are workable and probably overdue solutions in for the GCC, where lifestyle choices and driving are both health hazards.

If greed was good in the western financial markets, fat seems just as good in the EU.

Denmark recently became the first country to impose the dreaded 'fat' tax on butter, meats, milk, cheese, margarine and other 'fatty' foods. The new tax is designed to limit the Danes' intake of fatty foods. However, the Danes have decided to have their tax and eat it too. Sales of fatty foods rose steeply and locals hoarded up goodies before the price rise came into effect. To all accounts, fatty foods, otherwise chased by restless taste buds, have now acquired an additional attraction – as forbidden goodies.

Brave Heart Economics

Sub Saharan Africa ("SSA") today, is economically, where South East Asia ("SEA") was in the 1980s. SSA, however, is better placed with regard to inflation, foreign currency reserves, mineral resources and entrepreneurial spirit. SSA is currently labouring in the throes of striving for political and economic freedom from the NGO peddlers of democracy, which are usually the advance scouts of large businesses, a modus operandi of the divide (slice) and rule framework deployed by global business interests since the late 1500s, through Asia and, later in Eastern Europe and Caspian ring countries.

Real growth in SSA is expected to be consistently over 6.5 percent during the next two decades and several long running civil conflicts have come to an end. Nigeria for instance had fewer than 500,000 mobile telephone subscribers in the late 1990s and today has an estimated 35 million subscribers. Mobile telephones can and are being used in SSA to text air time back home, redeemable later for cash in a unique variation of modern micro fund transfers. Economic stability has seen private sector investment grow to around 30 percent of GDP with active participation from China, India, Russia, Brazil in addition to the UK and France. Indian entrepreneurs have for decades owned businesses in Kenya.

Key sectors with tremendous growth potential include mining, infrastructure, building materials, banking, retailing, insurance, pharmaceuticals/ healthcare, telecom, transportation, logistics, and soft commodities. Indeed SSA will benefit from both the fundamental and speculative advances in trading profiles of soft commodities across the globe. Exports from Nigeria, Kenya, Tanzania, Ghana, Uganda, Botswana and Mozambique include crude oil, natural gas, gold, cocoa, tea, coffee, sugar, textiles, platinum, tobacco, diamonds, nickel, and aluminium.

SSA exports to China are currently growing at over 30% year on year since 2000. SSA is experiencing a scramble of sorts by other countries to secure commodity supplies. This has also driven investments in infrastructure and logistics in the region. Foreign exchange reserves in SSA are now over USD 135bn, up from just USD 25bn in the late 1990s.

Equity markets in SSA countries offer diversified, attractive risk-adjusted returns. Zimbabwe, once freed from the shackles of western political adventurism, holds enormous potential for an economic upswing. Recent power sharing in Kenya has shown the way. SSA has over a dozen stock exchanges with at least 150 investment grade stocks and with an aggregate market capitalization estimated at nearly USD 100bn plus.

Recent upswings in the equities and property markets are also a product of Diaspora capital inflows – an estimated USD 50bn each year – another startling similarity to the developments in South East Asia in the 1970s/ 1980s (the "Kerala' factor for India). SSA economies have two other principal modern day advantages – investment opportunities for Islamic investment companies and SSA economies are insulated from threats of global warming. SSA is slated to be the global economic engine of this century and the next. Hunger? –Nearly 40% of New Yorkers (Bronx and Hispanic residents included) found it difficult in 2007 to put together the minimum daily calories consistently – that is a higher percentage than for SSA and Myanmar!!

SSA is now being drag pulled into the global economy, for want of sufficient growth markets globally. Until the early 1990s, Africa's GDP was higher than that of China's. However, by and large, the world media found it convenient to classify Africa as its 'misery' continent and the economic developments of the 1990s passed by Africa. China alone will invest an estimated USD 50bn in SSA between 2000 and 2012. It is not just Harrison Ford's Indiana Jones who has adventures in SSA.

BRIC and Mortar

With all the focus in recent months on the declining financial, consumer and labour markets in the west, the progress and gains in BRIC countries has largely gone by underreported. Around Moscow, warehouse type stores, mega malls and hypermarkets continue to mushroom in a rapidly expanding retail footprint. The boom has lasted for nearly a decade and Russia will probably become the largest consumer market for Europe. The expanding middle class, with their rising real income, has put 2012 first quarter retail sales growth forecasts at more than 10 percent. Over 50 percent of Henkel's (household products) global sales are from Russia.   France's Auchan (hypermarkets), PepsiCo and Danone are other examples of entrants that have been quick off the block. And, consumer credit, frowned upon now in many developed markets, is also on the upswing in Russia, helping to release pent up demand from Soviet era days.

Dim Sum bonds are bonds that are issued in Hong Kong and denominated in Yuan. Investors are usually based in Hong Kong or Singapore with the objective of developing Yuan denominated portfolio components. International fund managers, insurance companies and banks are also increasingly looking to participate in the Dim Sum bond market.   McDonald's is planning a second Yuan denominated bond issue and New Zealand dairy producer Fonterra has a 300 million Yuan offering. Raising funds in Chinese currency helps mitigate foreign exchange risks for companies with operations planned on the mainland. Caterpillar, Unilever and Volkswagen have also raised Yuan denominated debt. The growing size of Yuan bond issuances is no yawning matter. Nigeria recently announced its intentions to diversify at least 10 percent of its forex reserves into Chinese currency. While the US remains Nigeria's main investor and trading partner, Nigeria is clearly seeking to hedge its bets and attract low cost loans and investments from China.

Tomsk is a Siberian city with rows of gingerbread like brick and mortar houses. Tomsk is part of the strategy to diversify the Russian economy away from natural resources. One in five residents of Tomsk is a student and the city is now a university town with quality human resources. The city includes 200 hectares of techno parks and 10 business incubators. Incentives to companies setting up operations at Tomsk include exemptions from various value added taxes and customs duties, exemptions from property and transport taxes, reduced social taxes and profit taxes. Over USD 20 billion of innovative products were produced in 2010 at Tomsk. Recent breakthrough products include nano-bandages that help burns heal quicker.

Chile produces and exports a large variety of fruits as a consequence of the length of the country and its geographical diversity. The country's semi –desert regions and forests are a Garden of Eden. Chile's exports of fruit have grown by nearly 8 percent over 2010. Exports include apples, peaches, grapes, plums, avocados, kiwi fruit and berries. In addition to exports to North America, exports to Asian countries have grown by over 25 percent in 2011. Over 60 percent of fresh fruit exports from the southern hemisphere to the north are from Chile. Moving smartly up the value chain, Chile now exports processed fruit, paste, canned fruits and juices.

Employment news in the USA continues to get stranger by the month. Manufacturers have nearly 600,000 unfilled jobs as a result of a lack of skilled production workers. The shortage of a skilled workforce is hardly surprising, given that companies such as Microsoft, Oracle, Dell, Facebook and Disney, to name a few, were set up by dropouts. US workers with chronic health problems cost their economy over USD 150 billion each year in lost hours, and less than 15 percent are healthy (normal weight, no chronic illnesses).

Broken Windows

The USA's Sandy storm served to underline the classical 'broken window fallacy'. If a window is broken and then replaced, there is in fact no net benefit to the economy. Natural disasters or wars do not make the economy better rather only create an illusion of growth. The losses from destruction of property are not deducted from national gross domestic product. As a result of Sandy, sections of the US economy will look better because of the reconstruction work. However, way back in 1850, the French economist Bastiat explained the phenomenon with the 'broken window fallacy'. Bastiat was the first to explain that the net result of a natural disaster on an economy was negative. This is because, as Bastiat explained, there are a series of lost opportunities in terms of what else the reconstruction money could have funded. Bastiat was the first economist to underline the concept of opportunity costs. This also explains why the wars that the US has engaged in have always left the economy in a worse shape. A natural disaster can also lead to structural economic changes of a permanent nature. For example, residents moved out of New Orleans after hurricane Katrina, and businesses or individuals may decide to move out of New York because of the threat of floods.

Bastiat was known for his economic essays and parables which he used to explain economic theory. He made a strong case for free markets with his 'Candle makers' petition' parable. His candle makers present a petition to the French government to block out the sun because of the unfair competitive advantage. To illustrate that government trade restrictions are counter-productive he proposed that people should not be allowed to use their right hand. This would result in more difficulty, more work, and more employment. A parallel is the suggestion by some economists that a four day working week, would result in more employment. Bastiat is also known for his parable of the 'negative railroad'. In this parable, the governments of Spain and France should destroy the connecting railroad to prevent foreign goods from competing with locally produced goods – and destroying the railroad is a cheaper alternative economically than imposing import tariffs.

All economists have not been so fortunate. Nikolai Kondratieff published his ideas in 1925 relating to economic cycles that could last between 40 to 60 years. At the time, the Soviets did not believe that capitalism would last. Kondratiev was imprisoned and executed. In 1939, these business cycle patterns were named the Kondratieff waves by economist Schumpeter, a year after his execution. Kondratiev's theories of business cycles have now been proven to be correct. He explained long term business cycles in terms of demographic evolution (witness the recent elections in the USA), technological innovation, prices, interest rates, engineering developments, innovations in fuel and electricity generation (examples of the search for alternate fuel sources abound today), commodity price cycles, and most interestingly, he referred to a revolution in information and telecommunications (today's social media and mobile communications are good examples). The problem was that it was 1925, very few people believed Kondratiev's ideas, and he was treated as a trouble maker and criminal.

Demand and supply continue to be the foundations of economic theory. An estimated USD 6 billion was spent on the recent presidential election in the USA. The pumpkin centred Halloween festival, however, garnered spending of USD 8 billion in the economy, in a telling commentary on people's priorities. 72 percent of the US population participated in Halloween celebrations, far higher than the percentage of voter turnout. The pumpkin festival is now supported by significant corporate financial muscle, is one of the fastest growing holidays, is a major unifying factor across ages and all segments of society in the USA.

Burn Legacy

The good news is that humans do not have to worry (too much) about investment bankers, financial scams and economic crises. The not so good news, as Nobel laureate Schmidt has explained is that humans have bigger problems to worry about. Schmidt's studies explain that the sun is going to give out in 4 billion years and around 800 million years from now, it will probably be too hot for the earth. Schmidt shared the 2011 Nobel Prize in physics for also explaining that the universe continues to expand at a quicker pace and will eventually fade away into nothingness. It is extremely unlikely it appears that humans will ever find other life forms in the universe. Correspondingly, and happily so, it is also equally unlikely that extraterrestrial economic crises and financial scams will be brought home to earth by bankers.

Some corporations' revenues constitute a significant portion of the gross domestic product (GDP) of the countries in which they are domiciled. Nokia for example, was once paying over 20 percent of all Finnish corporation tax and generated a major portion of Finland's exports. Royal Dutch Shell's revenues are over 50 percent of the GDP of the Netherlands, ArcelorMittal's revenues are over 150 percent of Luxembourg's GDP and Essar Energy clocks in at 132 percent of the GDP of Mauritius. Nestle pulls its weight with revenues at almost 15 percent of Swiss GDP and a casino developer (Sands China) has sales that are 13 percent of Macao's GDP. Samsung, which has revenues twice that of Nokia, however, does not have a similar share in South Korea. These corporations could wield significant clout in terms of taxation policies, employment policies, and foreign direct investment policies in particular. However, they also bring with it, the risks of concentration resulting for the country of their domicile. Some countries just seem like larger corporate offices of global corporations.

In the USA, the cigarette companies have won the first round in their battle with the US Food and Drug Administration (FDA). A US court recently ruled that the FDA cannot force cigarette companies to put graphic health images on packaging. The US court ruled that there was insufficient evidence to show that the labels would reduce or prevent or deter smoking. The new warnings on cigarette packaging would have been the first significant change in cigarette health warnings in 25 years. The US court also stated that the images proposed by the FDA on packages, were much more than merely providing factual information to consumers. The FDA probably erred and undermined their case by relying on data from neighbouring Canada's use of graphic warning labels. Not surprisingly, the US court rejected the evidence from the Canadian study as 'underwhelming' and 'misleading. The US cigarette companies live to fight another day, the question on the table is, will their customers also live to fight another day?

Peter Thiel recently sold over 80 percent of his stake in Facebook and expressed frustration at the direction of development of social media. Thiel is a founder investor having lent Zuckerberg $500,000 initially, later converted to a 7 percent equity stake. He was also an early investor in LinkedIn and cofounded PayPal. Thiel's sale of his stake in Facebook has been likened to the pilot of a plane walking past the passengers, wearing a parachute. Peter Thiel's other interests include anti-ageing research. He has funded projects for DNA sequencing, cancer treatments and mobile applications that are designed to encourage healthy behavior (Thiel's objective is to extend the human lifespan beyond 100 years). Thiel believes in the power of innovation and technology. His now famous provocative scheme, offer $100,000 to students who will leave their university and work on start up ideas – a scholarship award for scholastic non-excellence.

(Total) Business Recalls

Global economies for much of the 20th century were divided along the lines of the 'haves' and 'have-nots'. In the 21st century the dividing economic line will probably those that are 'hungry for change' and those that are plain and simply 'hungry'. The meaning of some words in the English language does get 'recalled'. There was a time, not so long ago, when 'ERP' universally meant Enterprise Resource Planning. Students of the 21st century will know 'ERP' as Economic Rescue Package. 'ICBM', read as intercontinental ballistic missiles, now reads as international commodity black market.

Facebook was one of the biggest disappointments in 2011, for internet retailers and internet entrepreneurs alike. The social media platform simply did not deliver and the sales potential of social media networks appeared to be vastly overhyped. F-Commerce, as the bridge between social networks and internet shopping is called, did not take off and the runaway is looking a bit longer than expected. Social networks have been used as a brand exposure tool, to gather data about shoppers (as yet relatively unreliable) and to set up fully functional online stores within Facebook. Online retailers in the USA reported that barely half percent of customers were referred in through social networks.

The casual link between the 'Like' button and an actual sale is proving as elusive as the mystical Yeti figure that promised to conclusively prove the missing link between ape and man. Harvesting data from

Facebook's 'Like' function has not helped to point to potential sales. Clicking the 'Like' button is a compulsion for many Facebook users and is so common that it is referred to as 'Like-Bombing'. The Facebook friends of friends marketing crank shaft lever, relies on the soundness of the 'Like' polls and then basis social media marketing plans around how to entertain and engage the potential consumer base on a regular basis. For numerous reasons, not the least being the feature of lack of privacy, the social media marketing tractor beam is not proving to be an authentic indicator of customer preferences.

All that disappointment has not stopped investment firms from taking a long term call on investment opportunities. Kingdom Holding Company (KHC) recently acquired nearly 3 percent in Twitter for around USD 300 million. Twitter was classified by KHC as a high growth business with global impact potential and the investment was designated as a strategic stake. The other recent international investor in Twitter has been the Russian internet investment firm DST that shelled out around USD 400 million for a 5 percent stake in Twitter. In 1997, KHC took a 5 percent stake in Apple for a only USD 25 million and that stake is currently worth nearly USD 15 billion.

For commerce students, 'recall' meant memorizing business theory. For commerce students in the 21st century, 'recall' is more likely to refer to mass product recalls. Mass product recalls in the past 100 years have been carried out by companies such as Johnson and

Johnson, Firestone, Bridgestone, Toyota, Honda, Suzuki (Maruti) and recently by Indian automotive major Tata Motors. Product recalls send a signal of transparency and commitment to customers and are quickly becoming the benchmark of customer sensitive companies. Bicycles, automobiles and automotive parts, toys, apparel and pharma products were the main categories of recalls.

14 years on, after the Asian financial crisis, Indonesia has been recalled to investment grade. The rating upgrade will result in Indonesia's borrowing costs dropping further. The Indonesian economy is oriented toward domestic consumption, and is therefore, largely insulated from external slowdowns and shocks. The country's debt ratios, liquidity and conservative policy framework have all moved in the right direction. Further investments in infrastructure and improvements in the business climate (taxes, consumption stimulus, controls over corruption) should help improve the outlook.

Commercial Flash Dances

Frequent fliers in China are accustomed to frequent delays and frequent groundings. The proliferation of new airports, younger fleet and better services has not helped to improve punctuality. Less than 70 percent of flights arrive on time in China. Reasons include the confinement of non-governmental aircraft to narrow air corridors, inexperienced crews and inadequate management skills. Passengers have begun to stage protests on the runways by standing on the tarmac. The Chinese authorities have adopted a carrot and stick approach to quell passenger dissent. At some locations, police officers patrol check-in areas to control complaining passengers. Recently, travellers who were waiting for their flights to take off were entertained with refreshments and dancing cheerleaders – a first for airports worldwide. While training crews, improving management and privatization of airspace (less than 30 percent of Chinese airspace is free for civilian use) all can take decades, the authorities and the public are probably going to engage in competitive flash dances on Chinese tarmacs – the new age non-violent protests.

A 'cheapskate' is a person who will avoid paying a fair share, who has money but will not spend it, or having decided to spend will spend it on quantity instead of quality. Chesapeake Energy Corporation (the most active driller of wells in the US, leading producer of natural gas and a leader in oil field services) recently got matters a little mixed, showing that there is something after all in a name. Chesapeake had previously granted its CEO, founder well participation rights of up to 2.5

percent of all the company's wells. The program however, required the CEO to make large cash contributions ($ 1.01 billion between 2009 and the first quarter of 2012) and to make matters worse the CEO's salary was dropped by 15 percent in 2011. This left the CEO with a pile of debt against his stakes in the well. While natural gas prices have weakened upfront, investments in new wells continue to drain cash. The discounted value of earnings of the wells continued to decline and reached levels far below the debt on the CEO's table.

Chesapeake moved to end the grant of the grant of the 2.5 percent stake in the company's wells and the CEO's tenure as well, reneging on a promise that backfired. While more traditional stock options are frequently 'underwater' (market price less than the grant price), this is the first case of an employee option going underground literally. Shareholders at banks continue to protest non-violently and vote against executive management payouts. Citigroup, Barclays and UBS all recently faced shareholder dissent on executive compensation. Shareholder representatives are pushing for bank bonuses to be more closely aligned with profit and stock performance, and risk management. The votes of dissent, however, are non-binding and it is not inconceivable that shareholders in the US may eventually follow the example of Chinese airport authorities and flash dance their way into general body meetings.

More interesting occupations (than expressing dissent in novel ways) actually exist in this decade. The job of 'piracy risk analyst' ('PRA') is fast developing into a worthwhile occupation. A PRA (as opposed to a PRO) uses data from events, weather forecasts and debriefs from captives (released) to predict the possible incidence of future pirate attacks on the high seas. Ships in transit, in the likely line of fire are provided with alerts and shipping lines are assisted with planning routes. PRAs are typically ex naval navigating officers with some experience in the Indian Ocean. The growing incidence of piracy attacks in that region makes the Bermuda triangle look friendly and bemused in comparison. Not far beyond this occupation is surely related insurance and tax planning (for corporate payments of ransom made to pirates – presumably, pirates do not file tax returns).

Coutt, Un Coutt

Coutt & Co. ('Coutt') is the private bank used by Britain's Queen Elizabeth II. A probe by the Financial Services Authority resulted in a fine of £12.5 mn (discounted by 30 percent for early settlement). Coutt violated money laundering regulations and did not carry out stipulated checks on a majority of its clients with 'politically exposed' positions or clients vulnerable to corruption. The FSA concluded that there had been an unacceptable risk that the bank may have handled proceeds of crime. The bank failed in identifying high risk clients and in adequately monitoring transactions (in some instances, criminal links were identified, but not followed up and customers were approved). Coutt's problems stemmed from around 2007 when the bank promoted bonus policies based on number of customers signed up. According to FSA, Coutt's failings were significant, widespread and unacceptable. The private bank used by the Queen is now an example of uncouth behaviour by a private bank.

By next year, it could get worse. The Queen's head could fall into private hands. The government in the UK has set a date for the privatization of the Royal Mail. The Royal Mail is clearly not equipped to compete in a digital environment, has a unionized workforce and owes an obligation to provide delivery to all parts of the UK within an affordable price structure. Price controls and a pension funding gap of over £9 billion are the other key problems faced by the Royal Mail. There are hopes that either a full or partial sell off will bring in much needed funds for new investments, bring in efficiencies and help compete in the more profitable segments of information delivery and messaging. Meanwhile, the Encyclopaedia Britannica is going out of print after 244 years. Only 8,000 sets of the 2010 edition were sold (120,000 in 1990). Print encyclopaedias contribute less than 1 percent of Britannica's revenues. A majority of the company's revenues now is based on sales of curriculum products in English, science and math. The math clearly does not add up and print editions have been submerged by the internet revolution. Web sites such as Wikipedia are easier to update and far more easily accessible. Martians visiting Earth will have to look beyond the gold lettered Encyclopaedia (with its 32 volumes) to learn about human kind.

It was not so long ago that the IMF was burdened with a head that has a political background and no background in economics. The US President is going one better, with his nominee for the head of the World Bank. Jim Yong Kim ('JYK') is a Korean – American physician and president of Dartmouth College. JYK has an MD from Harvard Medical School and has a history of focus on radical, community focused health care programs. JYK is on record as being anti-growth. His hypothesis is that corporate led economic growth tends to make the middle class and the poor worse off. He has few views, if any on economic policy and his focus has been on health policy and programs. JYK believes that the quest for increasing GDP has worsened the lives of millions. The circle of global economic mess is almost complete.

The head of IMF is a politician who does not understand economics and the proposed head of World Bank is a physician who is anti-growth. All the US Treasury needs is a poet (of Chinese origin) and the UK, a Chancellor - painter (of African origin).

The United Arab Emirates continues to find new means of attracting tourists. The Real Madrid Resort Island (to open in 2015) will have 50 hectares including a 10,000 capacity sea facing stadium, museum, theme park and training academy, and is expected to attract one million tourists a year – branded sand, what's next?

Critical Mess

Business valuation methodologies had two cornerstones for discounting projected cash flows. A risk free discounting rate that would then be built up to account for country, sector and transaction specific risks, and a terminal growth factor to approximate the value of cash inflows to perpetuity (usually at a long term growth rate of two to three percent). Today, post the global sovereign debt crises, the concept of risk free rate (previously anchored around the ten year US Treasury rate) is redundant since sovereign debt is no longer risk free. Similarly, counter parties are reluctant to recognize a terminal value with growth to perpetuity assumption because of the rapidly changing economic horizon and an inability to look beyond the short term. In some segments, however, business valuations are prospering.

A new class of business valuations brings to mind the cinematic sword and shield drama '300'. SAP recently acquired Success Factors for $3.4 billion and Oracle bought up Right Now for $1.5 billion. Both companies are pushing initiatives to deliver all weather, cloud based delivery of software via internet and this is expected to reduce hardware costs of customers. Valuations of cloud based start-ups are reaching sky high. Success Factors was bought out by SAP at 333 times its earnings. In terms of multiples of net sales, companies developing cloud based services, fetch valuations of between six to nine times next year's sales. Attractive metrics when growth rates are on cloud nine, for example, Success Factors recently had third quarter sales growth of nearly seventy percent.

A principal benefit of the current global economic and funding outage has been the expansion of our concepts of what is financially possible and what is economically impossible e.g. it has surprised many that it is economically impossible to carry on borrowing indefinitely without adequate capacity to repay and without a significant increase over time on the cost of borrowing. Indeed, the fact that borrowing at a sovereign level has finite limits had been forgotten. It has also become abundantly clear that the more complex financial markets become, the more difficult it is to remedy in times of distress or breakdown.

Prof. Ian Morris at Stanford had devised an index of social development that hinted that society has developmental limits. The index was constructed around a few principal criteria such as capacities in the fields of energy capture (access to food, fuel and power), organization of society referenced by city size (witness the development of early stage Greek and Roman cities), communications technologies and the capacity to wage war (witness China's recent attempts to project its military prowess far beyond its borders). Prof. Morris's research and theories led him to believe that every society eventually reached a point of stagnation, bottleneck and degeneration resulting from warfare, scarcity of resources or unsustainable degradation of the geophysical environment including climate, water or disease. Every 'empire' had and will have its own Dark Ages.

China's gross domestic product fell rapidly between 1820 and 1870 and then again between 1914 and the late 1940s. Russia's economy collapsed by over 40 percent following the Reagan-Gorbachov engineered collapse of communism in the 1990s. Periodic economic catastrophe appears to be inevitable and societies have a natural sequence of events and a ceiling of development. History, it seems does not merely repeat itself, but repeats itself with unfailing regularity and at reasonably predictable intervals. Social and financial structures do not keep pace with development, leading to bottlenecks, then slowdowns and finally declines in every major geography and society. Creation of artificial scarcities of valued resources and degradation of the environment emerge as the core competencies of human society and business firms. Critical mass to critical mess is not such a long route after all.

Custo Undo

The workshop of the world, the British Midlands, is finding new ways to recover lost ground and compete with low cost Asian manufacturers. A weaker sterling pound and slowly rising wages in South East Asia have helped the recovery. Long distance supply chains have also been affected by natural disasters. Support networks such as Supply Chain 21 help to spread around best practices, raising efficiencies, lowering costs and improving quality. Business networks such as Made in the Midlands supports members by sharing knowledge and solving problems. Employment in the Midland is up, although the UK continues to steadily lose manufacturing jobs.

UK is turning off wind farm electricity. Plenty is not good when it comes to wind power. National Grid paid out over £12 million in compensation to wind farm operators. High-speed winds overload power grids and wind powered turbines are switched off. UK's grids have struggled to receive and channel power generated by wind farms and the networks are often overloaded with wind power. The alternative technologies (tidal, wind and solar) and energy sources are available, the problem being that the write offs in traditional power generation systems (from fossil fuels) would be huge. Similarly, automobile companies have the technology to produce economical, environmentally clean vehicles. But then, what will they do with the investments in gas guzzling engines?

Brazil's gross domestic product grew by less than 3 percent in 2011. The problems of the EU (Brazil's key trading partner), have directly impacted the economy. Brazil, however, is now the world's sixth largest economy, ahead of the UK. The government continues to struggle with balancing inflation, lending rates, growth rates, pension reform, reducing levels of corruption, rationalizing the tax regime and government spending. The sharp rise in the currency has also damaged commodity and manufacturing exports. Government spending flows mainly into state payrolls and this limits the capacity to fund developments in infrastructure, education and health. The cost of doing business ('Custo Brasil') in Brazil is high, taxation and welfare policies do not help.

Lenovo, the world's second largest maker of computers, following its purchase of the IBM line, recently reported growth in sales by over 40 percent. Lenovo's share price has risen by over 35 percent in the past year and sales in mature markets grew by 80 percent. Its market share of China's personal computer market is over thirty percent. Lenovo's price to earnings multiple is twice that of global leader HP, higher than both Dell and even Apple. CEO Yang now has the pockets to take on development losses as Lenovo attempts to expand into smart phones, tablets and smart TVs. Demand for laptops is facing a fierce onslaught from tablets and the PC market no longer looks secure. HP, meanwhile, faces tough times ahead. In recently reported results, a majority of HPs large operating segments showed earnings decline by at least 30 percent. HP has lost significant market share in both PC and server segments, and is grappling with the dilemma of short term profits versus spending on innovation (only 2.5 percent of revenues) and marketing to ensure long term sales growth. Unlike IBM and Dell, HP's transformation does not have a rebuild model. IBM shifted focus to software and services and Dell moved to corporate computing and services.

The Bank of France will book a profit of nearly 500 million Euros thanks to citizens who hoarded the franc and did not swap them for Euros or not having paid taxes on their income just did not cough up their francs. The French franc was effectively discontinued recently, and the currency created for Jean "le Bon" in 1360 (as his ransom after a defeat in 1356) is no longer legal tender. Real world business does not often have an 'undo' button.

Expendable Entrepreneur-sheep

Wu Ying at one point was the richest woman in China. The Chinese entrepreneur made a fortune selling sheep extract as an anti-wrinkle cream. This line of business and entrepreneurship ('Entrepreneur-sheep') was solidly supported by the authorities. Wu Ying, however turned to investing and asset management. In China, the financial system is dominated by state run entities and it is illegal to run investment activities without governmental approvals. Wu Ying was found guilty of illegally collecting funds and was sentenced to death. The Supreme Court later reversed the ruling in appeal and put Wu Ying down for life imprisonment. The public uproar supported her cause, since private investment companies had become a nationwide practice by the time her appeal came up before the Supreme Court. China seems to have got it right, in terms of sentencing of fund managers who lose other people's money without remorse. However, it does seem strange that selling sheep extract as anti-wrinkle cream is not a crime – maybe the cream works best for the sheep. Judging by the marketing success of the cream, 'Ba Ba Black Sheep' do you have any cream, is likely to be the newer version of the nursery rhyme.

The two oldest questions around have now been joined by a third. For long people have asked why the chicken crossed the road and how many electricians does it take to change a light bulb. These two questions have now been joined by a third universal question since 2009. How many bankers does it take to take a company public? Recently, PICC, the Chinese insurer, got as many as 14 banks working on its $ 6 billion sale of

67

shares. The banks stand any chance of earning a fee only if they rope in Cornerstone investors, who get allotments and accept a lock in period. Hong Kong is now the world's largest shares listing market, and Cornerstones take up to thirty percent of the listings in Hong Kong. Approaching a dozen banks and pre-selling portions of the IPO appears to be the way forward in a risky market.

The movie industry has witnessed a couple of movies that have lumped together a motley collection of ageing heroes and stars (Avengers puts together Hulk, Iron Man, Thor, Captain America and the Expendables sequel promises to do worse). The business world can hardly be far behind. The two best known groups in Europe and the US will now come together in a strategic partnership. Rothschild and Rockefeller are now putting together a deal that will allow RIT to acquire 37 percent in Rockefeller's wealth advisory and asset management group. David Rockefeller is 96 and Lord Rothschild is 76. The question is, are these the new Avengers or the new Expendables of the business world?

Farmers in India's north western dry, arid, blindingly hot desert regions stand to benefit hugely from the developments in the shale energy industry in the US and Europe. Guar, a bean, has long been used as an input to make sauces and ice cream. It turns out that Guar is also a significant ingredient in the process of hydraulic fracturing, essential to shale energy. Guar has turned into black gold for the farmers and prices in 2012 have risen by ten times in the past year alone. India is the biggest producer of Guar in the world, with a current crop of one million tonnes of the beans each year. India's large producers of guar gum are distributing seeds free to farmers. Ice cream producers are likely to suffer a rise in input costs and farmers in other deserts around the world will keenly look to grow the beans. It certainly looks as if any which way, black gold is to be found in the deserts on this planet.

Fat Cats

The weight management industry clocks over $ 10 billion in retail sales each year. The diet and weight watch aids industry has always been extremely innovative. Powders that signal a full stomach to the brain, sprays that curb craving for food and powders that block absorption of fat or calories by the cells, stomach constricting devices are only some of the industry's many innovations. One pill, 'Qnexa' promises to melt body weight. Financial markets must be hoping to take a leaf from the book of the weight management industry. A pill that would melt debt and non-performing assets, a powder that would signal high levels of borrowings or sprays that would curb shareholder cravings for profits or management cravings for bonus payouts would be welcomed by the business community and governments.

FATCA is a more serious problem for the wealthy. Not to be confused with Fat Cats, FATCA (Foreign Account Tax Compliance Act) impacts those with obese bank balances. While Buffett continues to soft campaign for higher taxes on the wealthy, over 1,700 people gave up their US nationality in 2011 (only 235 in 2008). The US levies taxes on global income of its citizens. Strict asset disclosure rules under FATCA, disclosure of foreign financial assets, shareholdings in on US companies and other provisions including withholding taxes on US connected payments has made personal tax planning incredibly difficult. A $450 fee, an exit tax and a less than ten minute renunciation interview is all that it takes to give up US citizenship. Post FATCA, Swiss and

German banks are no longer safe tax havens for Americans. Meanwhile, the Gini Index in the US shows that the genie is well and truly out of the bottle. Inequalities in distribution of income are at all time high levels, seen before only during the 1920s and 1930s. The economic crises have lent credence to the theory that income inequalities leads inevitably to declining economic performance.

The issue of whether to tax the rich more is hotly debated in the US. One school of thought subscribes to the view that people are either already wealthy or wanting to be wealthy, and neither category wants higher taxes. There is little empirical evidence, from the days of Robin Hood and his merry men, that taxing the rich has solved the problem of inequalities in distribution of income. Income inequality is generally a good social motivator and generates aspirations, ambition and private enterprise. In extremes, with a high Gini Index, it can be a socially divisive factor. However, almost anything in extremes is destructive of social fabric.

It may surprise people to learn that Sony is essentially currently a Japanese banking and insurance company. For long known as an electronics and entertainment company, Sony plans to cut 10,000 jobs and continue to scale back its highly unprofitable television manufacturing businesses. Banking and insurance generates more profits for Sony than music, mobile phones, music, films combined. Other old school companies however, continue to soldier along.

Companies such as Dow Chemicals, Colgate – Palmolive, Kellogg, ExxonMobil and other old school companies have solid traditions of dividend payouts. The strength of their brands allows them to increase retail selling prices to offset rising material costs and to generate organic sales growth. Globally diversified companies with strong brands are also better equipped to withstand regional economic downturns.

For 'new age' businesses lacking brand equity, the European crises, falling demand in China, rising commodity prices, lack of consumer confidence, lack of investor confidence, rising interest rates, foreign exchange fluctuations, over capacity, slump in real estate are some of the management excuses finding their way into investor reports. Meanwhile, as the Olympics draws nearer, Greece spreads its own flaming torch of economic tribulation through Spain, Portugal and Italy in a macabre relay.

Faustian Creative Destruction

Cope's Rule states that in the evolution of animals, lineages get larger over time. Edward Cope's 19th century theory explained that over time, evolution tends to make animals larger however, since larger animals need more resources, the species is eventually rendered vulnerable. The 21st century has shown that Cope's Rule applies to economies, governments and corporations as well. 'Schumpeter's Gale' (also known as 'creative destruction') was drawn from the works of Karl Marx. Marxist economic theory described the processes of accumulation and destruction of wealth under capitalism. Karl Marx admired the creativity and innovation of capitalism, but considered its self-destruction inevitable. Schumpeter's theory considered creative destruction cycles as normal costs of business under capitalism. It appears that large enterprises are destined to eventually fail.

E.F. Schumacher's award winning book 'Small is Beautiful: Economics As If People Mattered', opposed 'bigger is better'. Schumacher was a firm believer of 'production by the masses' instead of 'mass production'. Too often, government activity has expanded into almost every sphere of enterprise. Most public services (airlines, household water/ gas, telecommunications, media, post, even garbage collection) are better off, financially and in service levels, when privatized. Tax pools and government enterprise in developed economies have grown exponentially. Governmental taxes for household services have often led to much dissatisfaction. Co-operatives and contributions applied locally to services provided by private enterprise (with competitive bidding), usually works better (e.g. garbage collection, internet services). Larger governments are more than likely to fulfil Cope's Rule.

A Faustian bargain is one in which a person gives up something precious to achieve what would otherwise be unattainable. Faustian bargains are common to both German legends and Polish folklore ('Pan Twardowski'). In one 19th century drama, a bankrupt emperor is persuaded to print and spend huge amounts of money to solve his problems with the predictable ending of chaos. The quantitative easing in Western economies is a true Faustian bargain – it solves nothing and only postpones the inevitable without solid structural reforms. Tragically, people and their leaders have nearly always looked for short term fixes.

Small and medium businesses ('SMEs') in the UK are now forced to look overseas, to develop their business prospects. The economy of the UK is fragile and will probably remain so for at least the next 5 years. Dan Bobby, CEO of Calling Brands believes that relying on the UK market alone is dangerous for small businesses in the UK. SMEs in the UK are the heart of the economy and help keep employment numbers up, and are aggressively looking to expand in Europe and in the USA. Waiting for the economy to improve is no longer an option for British businesses. Firms offering website design, online marketing tools, social media tools and communication tools for SMEs are looking at an upswing in opportunities with businesses in the UK.

The Financial Services Authority in the UK ('FSA') has declared its intention to limit the marketing of investments such as fine wine, classic cars, overseas property etc. Only experienced investors, those who earn more than £ 100,000 annually or have over £ 250,000 to invest would be able to participate in such investment schemes. Unfortunately, investors who have already placed money in 'unregulated collective investment schemes ('UCIS') will take losses, as the new rules, scheduled to come in from 2013, will reduce the liquidity of such investments. Meanwhile, people in Dublin are eagerly buying up theatre tickets for a new production 'Anglo: The Musical'. The Anglo is a satire on Ireland's economic bust up that began initially with the fall of the Anglo Irish Bank. The tag line is that it takes only a few 'muppets' to cause financial chaos for an entire country (together with a dash of Faustian blunders and a dash of creative destruction).

Financially In Orbit

Mrs. Watanabe is the generic name for Japanese housewives who speculate or invest in foreign exchange instruments. Watanabe is the fifth most common Japanese family name and the Watanabe Samurai were a highly respected class. The term 'Mrs. Watanabe' is the personification of Japanese housewife investors, who collectively, wield financial strength sufficient to influence foreign exchange markets. According to the Bank of Japan, Mrs. Watanabe has financial assets more than USD 18 trillion. In pursuit of better yielding financial instruments, Japanese housewives provide capital to foreign issuers. The current favourite of Mrs. Watanabe is the Turkish lira. Uridashi bonds are foreign currency denominated bonds sold to Mrs. Watanabe. Sales of lira linked Uridashi bonds topped USD 2 billion in the first six months of 2012. Yields on Turkish bonds are currently one of the most attractive. In the past year alone, Mrs. Watanabe has withdrawn over USD 30 billion from Brazilian-real exposed funds. This retreat from the Brazilian-real is symptomatic of many things wrong with Brazil's economy.

Reduction in Brazil's benchmark interest rates, capital controls, transaction taxes on trading in derivatives have all contributed to Mrs. Watanabe's withdrawals. As Brazil heads toward the Olympic games of 2016, the Brazilian economy suffers from a national crisis of confidence. Brazilians are asking whether the 2016 Games will do to Brazil what the 2004 Games did to Greece. The Brazilian economy is not internationally competitive and infrastructure is poor. Brazil is one of the largest exporters of iron ore and yet it is cheaper to import steel made in South Korea. The cost of exporting a container from Brazil is twice that of China. In an amazing display of lack of self-belief in its competitiveness, Brazil's champion football club's recent recruit was a young Chinese footballer from Guangzhou.

The number of patent disputes in the UK has risen by nearly 200 percent. The recessionary economic climate has resulted in business owners proactively resorting to litigation to secure their intellectual property, designs and market share. In contrast, when the economy is performing well, businesses find patent litigation not worth the trouble to pursue, considering the somewhat uncertain outcomes. An increasing number of businesses are now turning to court action to protect and enforce the patents that they own. Patent court action is far more prevalent in the context of technology based industries. Google's purchase of Motorola last year for nearly USD 10 billion was driven in part by the estimated 25,000 patents attached to the sale.

The 30th Olympics is the first Olympics where a Village has gone bankrupt even before the end of the Games. At least one Village (hospitality centre), located at the Kensington Gardens, near the Royal Albert Hall was forced to close due to mounting debts. The business case for permanent Olympic Games sites and for the Games to be held every 2 years (instead of 4), is strong. London witnessed a large number of pop-up restaurants and supper clubs catering to dinner parties and serving food from various countries. Pop-up food at temporary sites (including trucks), were supported by social networks and private booking systems. Popular pop-ups such as supper clubs 'Eat the Olympics', 'Global Feast', 'Pizza Pilgrims', and 'Forza Win' provided Olympic-themed culinary delights.

Before the end of the Olympics, having lost the battle with 'chicken *tikka masala*' (Britain's national dish), the British PM Mr. Cameron has complained about the time spent on Indian dance at British schools. Britain is still smarting from the Orbit fiasco. The UK's largest piece of strange public art was designed and financed by Indian born artist and business tycoon. The Orbit's uniquely atrocious design has relegated the UK's Stonehenge to second place in the category of strange socio-business misadventures, and is guaranteed to mystify visitors for another 4,000 years.

Fine Regimes

The EU is rapidly becoming a 'fine' regime. In addition to the fines up to ten percent of revenue that it can levy to regulate fair competition (Intel and Microsoft have taken early hits), the EU plans to levy fines up to five percent of global revenue on companies that breach privacy rules. The new data protection legislation seeks to protect data of customers, suppliers and even employees. Companies that sell data to third parties without authorization or companies that do not protect data held in social networks or cloud computing bases will face heavy fines. The EU has already levied fines to nearly €2 billion with regard to regulation of competition and the proposed privacy legislation will to raise several billions more in fines – a fine pickle for firms in the EU to fin(e)d themselves in.

Equity or risk capital is likely to be one commodity in short supply in the 21st century. The accumulation of wealth in emerging markets, more particularly in CARB (Canada, Australia, Russia and Brazil) and BRICQ (Brazil, Russia, India, China and Qatar) markets is accompanied by write downs of equity interests in the developed economies. The supply of global equity is also affected by aging populations in the larger economies, stern regulatory provisions, accounting standards and dwindling returns on equity markets. Meanwhile, in emerging economies, private households have a preference for bank and company deposits, government bonds and savings schemes, versus equity investments.

A smaller proportion of emerging market private investments finds its way to equities as compared with developed markets. Of the total global financial assets, only around 25 percent is currently held by emerging or developing economies. By 2020, this will more likely rise to 35 percent, with a correspondingly lower proportion of global financial assets in equity markets. For example, in China, the household equity allocation of financial assets is around 15 percent only, whereas corresponding percentages of equity allocation are as high as 40 percent in the US and 30 percent in the EU. Another major factor impacting the slowdown of equity funding, is that worldwide insurers are off loading equity positions to comply with new regulatory capital requirements. Insurers are likely to dispose over $150 billion of equity holdings by end 2015. All of this will lead to a shortage of funding of growth capital and a fall in premiums on equity offerings as promoters chase the one commodity shortage (equity funding) most likely to outstrip the energy crises.

While on the subject of fine regulation, HSBC was recently fined £10.5 million and ordered to pay £29.3 million in compensation, by the UK's FSA (financial services authority). HSBC was deemed guilty of offloading inappropriate financial products to thousands of elderly clients in the UK. The average ages of these clients was over eighty, and most were too old or too ill to realize any benefits from these products. The fine is the largest ever in FSA annals for retail misdeeds and HSBC's CEO expressed 'profound' regrets while being criticized for taking unfair financial advantage of trusting elderly people. Brutal mugging, it appears no longer takes place on street corners, although the elderly remain the softest targets.

Meanwhile, in cinema woodland, Puss in Boots (a lisping Antonio Banderas) has joined the ranks of legendary comic strips figures Phantom (and wolf), Lothar and others who dare to drink milk in roughneck saloons. It is also the first successful pussy (or catty) movie that does not rely on a mouse or dog to prop the feline story line – unusually, in a first for feline cinema, it has a rather over boiled egg (supposedly Humpty Dumpty) holding up the at times, marginally drooping shenanigans of the gloved cat in boots.

Flavours of Innovation

Recently, Iran's judiciary passed out four death sentences, two life imprisonment sentences and sentenced over thirty persons to prison terms ranging up to 25 years. The perpetrators of the alleged crimes encouraged bank managers to provide loans and letters of credit that were used innovatively to purchase stakes in state owned companies. Financial systems have seen few socially useful innovations over time. Paul Volcker a former Fed Chairman once said that the ATM (first installed in London in 1967) was probably the most significant financial invention in 25 years. Banking was first developed around 3,000 BC in Mesopotamia, the first stock exchange established in 1602 in Amsterdam and the first mutual fund launched in the Netherlands in 1774. The launch of the independent microfinance Grameen bank in 1983 marked one of the few financial innovations that shouldered social responsibility.

Historically, most financial innovations have been used to spread or take on avoidable exposures to risks, in some cases, even to produce undesirable risks. Nobel laureate Joseph Stiglitz stated that most financial innovation 'was not directed at enhancing the ability of the financial sector to perform its social functions'. Social impact bonds are an interesting, yet unproven innovation. Impact investing links payouts to outcomes and aligns investors' objectives with the interests of various parties, and is especially useful to support government programs.

Humble shop floor engineering has absorbed innovation at a much faster rate than financial markets. Watson Steel, a Lancashire steelworks has helped put together structures such as London's Olympic Park's twisted 'Orbit', Birmingham's Bullring, the Millennium in Gateshead, airports in Hong Kong, Osaka and Paris. What is unusual about Watson Steel is that its 'workshop' includes a medieval style milling machine, laser beams, a laptop, an old fashioned camera, a software package refined by lens manufacturer Leica, and a theodolite perched on a tripod. Watson Steel's boutique engineering works with a 3D model in its fabrication workshop that translates architect's or artist's designs directly to the shop floor. Each hole, weld and the relative position of each piece of metal are precisely calculated – with a small margin of error.

The one financial innovation that could have contributed significantly was much abused with predictable disastrous consequences. The late Marion Sandler was a pioneering banker and generous philanthropist. Sandler developed a financial institution that once held $125 billion in assets, $60 billion in deposits, nearly 300 offices and 12,000 employees. Marion Sandler designed the innovative lending practice of adjustable rate mortgages ('pick-a-pay') which enabled lower income borrowers to choose payment plans based on what they could afford. The difference between Sandler's Golden West Financial and other financial intermediaries was that Sandler did not practice bundled securitisation of debt and stayed within the boundaries of prudential lending practices.

Sandler who was known to knit scarves at meetings, was one of the first women to head a Fortune 500 company, and was a keen supporter of The Center for Responsible Lending, Human Rights Watch, the American Civil Liberties Union and investigative journalism, besides having signed up to Buffet's Giving Pledge. Would Marion Sandler have been better at scarves and ice cream?–one never knows.

The ice cream manufacturing industry has also demonstrated more innovation (much of it also being socially appreciated). The industry has supplemented the all time favourites of vanilla, strawberry and chocolate, with flavours such as Heston Blumenthal's mustard ice cream, Humphrey Slocombe's salt & pepper, peanut-butter-curry, Robin Weir's recommended ricotta, goat's cheese, Morfudd Richard's crab, horseradish, and Lanterna's black pudding flavours. The Persians, Chinese and the Roman Emperor Nero were variously credited with the first variations of ice cream. The Vietnamese coconut milk Pandan waffles topping the list. However, it was the Arabs who were the first to use milk, sugar and initiate commercial production of ice cream.

Four Casts

Ignorance is bliss has long held sway as a phrase with deep merits. Hong Kong's financial secretary once held the opinion that the office of national statistics should be abolished. The absence of employment statistics was seen as a remedy to help poorer nations along the path to prosperity. Two key problems were seen to arise from the compilation and publishing of statistics. One, poor economic data generally gained momentum and became self-prophecies, spreading doom and gloom. Secondly, statistics strengthened the hand of governments to interfere in free markets, and universally, this has never been held to be a good thing for the economy. Thirdly, statistics (as in the case of Greece) often tell only a part of the story, can be manipulated and sometimes are plain cooked.

Economists too, are notoriously poor at forecasting. History has shown that economists do not have a much better record than the average investor in forecasting. Economic forecasts are as much of a science as weather forecasts. For example, the only predictable aspect about most central bankers' forecasts is that they will be revised each quarter. Most famously, three days before the crash of 1929, economist Fisher stated confidently that the stock markets had reached a permanently high plateau. Paul Samuelson held the view that economists predicted nine of the preceding five recessions. The Bank of England's forecasts have been changing with unfailing regularity. Trust in forecasts is often misplaced, and the Bank of England, inexplicably made questionably emergency loans to the Royal Bank of Scotland and HBOS. Similarly, its policies of injecting liquidity were designed with the objective of preventing future, 'forecasted' crises, rather than solving the immediate crisis at hand. The Bank of England's court of directors has recently commissioned an independent investigation into the forecasting capabilities of the Monetary Policy Committee. What most experienced investors could have told them, without an investigation, is that 'forecasting' capabilities, quite simply are a myth.

In the long term scheme of things, Japan's economic growth in the 20th century, appears now to have been a flash in 'the pan'. Japan is desperately trying to stimulate the economy using export subsidies and government spending. Key economic ailments facing Japan are the shortage of power (definitely not resolved with nuclear power plants), an export dependent economy (China is learning the very same lesson currently), an ageing population, rising social security costs, inadequate child care, astronomical levels of public debt (200 percent of annual gross domestic product), wealthy cash hoarders, rising consumption taxes, low women's participation in the workforce, inflexibility on employment of post retirement workers etc. The Bank of Japan has shown itself to be completely out of sync with developments in financial markets. In the midst of the current financial crises, the Bank of Japan has set itself and inflation goal of one percent. If Japan does not change its course, the country is headed for yet another Chapter 11 (country 11) in the next decade, following the path laid out by Greece, Spain, Portugal, Italy and other illustrious developed countries.

Politicians of today debate between austerity measures, growth, inflation, currency values, and employment. These are conflicting objectives only to politicians in terms of their commitments to vote banks, and are not conflicting objectives in economic terms. The French philosopher Jean Buridan's philosophy of moral determinism was illustrated with the example of 'Buridan's donkey, that when placed equidistant from a stack of hay and a pail of water, died of both hunger and thirst, as a result of inability to make any rational decision. The massive crises in the Euro zone have also been compared with the infamous Schleswig-Holstein question. Lord Palmerston declared that only three persons possessed the answer to the Schleswig-Holstein question, and they were dead, mad and with a failed memory.

Funny Money & the Bull Run

It has been confirmed that the financial chicken did come before the egg. Debt did come before 'money'!! An anthropologist Graeber, in his book on the first 5,000 years of debt explains how credit records were in place as far back as 3,000BC in Mesopotamia. This was before 'money' and 'currency' evolved. Money (bullion based money used by the Romans and Chinese) emerged as a medium of exchange much later than credit. Debtors were subservient to the social power of their creditors. Today, conversely, debtor nations are considered 'developed' and their creditor nations of the East are considered 'developing' or 'poor'. Statistics, however, don't usually lie, unless interpreted fancifully. In parallel with the high levels of debt in America, recent studies have shown that over 15 percent (nearly 46.5 million) Americans are living below the poverty line, the highest since 1993.

Reagan was quoted as saying that governments do not solve problems, instead, they subsidize them. Recent economic difficulties in Europe have given a boost to socialist policies and politicians. Spanish socialists propose a wealth tax to help spread the difficulties of austerity measures. French socialists have proposed that employee stock options should be banned, rating agencies be abolished, speculation on sovereign debt banned, creation of public sector jobs for the youth and that higher protectionist customs barriers should be erected. Globalization, after all, it seems, is not such a good thing, especially if it benefits developing countries.

In 1972, nearly 200 years on, the Chinese prime minister, Chou En Lai was reported to have remarked that it was too early to assess the impact of the French revolution (1789) on western civilization. Likewise, it is perhaps too early to assess the economic impact of GATT, the formation of the EU and WTO (1995), all three of which were designed to push open markets in Africa and the East to western economies. Felipe Gonzalez a former Spanish socialist prime minister who led Spain into the EU, recently said that EU member states, in trying to solve their problems of national debt, were like greyhounds chasing the elusive mechanical hare that they have no hope of catching.

An agile and intelligent bull named 'Mouse' has given Spaniards a run for their money and a bull run that has nothing to do with their stock markets. Mouse has over 3,000 fans and a rock star like following in Sueca, Valencia. Insurance agents, journalists and various animal rights groups are also following his adventures. The 11 year old Mouse is due to retire undefeated after a six year career in the ring and is valued at over half a million dollars. Mouse would probably have enjoyed Martin Scorsese's 1980, Jake La Motta based, sports film 'Raging Bull'. While Mouse ruminates over his next run, investors worldwide are skipping back and forth across the stock market line that runs between bullish and foolish.

Immigrant inflows have significantly reversed during the past year as a result of unemployment woes in various countries. Britain's migration cap, Poland's pilot scheme to reduce incomers, Denmark's border controls, Spain and Japan's 'pay to go away' compensation for workers who agree to return home, France's controls on Romanian immigrants and Australia's efforts to amend their constitution to allow authorities to ship immigrants to Malaysia – are all examples of recent shutters down policies on immigration. College graduates are increasingly likely to leave America, Britain and the EU to find work with companies in Asia, or China. Eastward travelling Americans may be surprised to learn that Eran, far from being in the 'Middle East', is in fact an ancient Indian city, a commercial capital, producing coins as far back as the 3rd century BC.

Gaian Hypotheses

The Gaia hypothesis proposes that organisms interact with their surroundings, influence their environment and develop to form self-regulating systems. The hypothesis was formulated by James Lovelock in the 1970s and is used in disciplines such as ecology, climate science and geo-physiology. Gaian hypotheses, apparently applies equally to the business world as well, and businesses evolve continuously, interacting with the social and business environment in which they operate. Japanese companies take into account the blood group of prospective candidates at the time of recruitment. Ketsu-eki-gata (the blood type theory) attempts to define the correlation between the various blood types, personality traits, and therefore, suitability for various forms of employment.

Blood group' A' is stated to be a gentle, modest person, willing to make sacrifices, while being meticulous, systematic, honest, and organized. Blood group 'O' on the other hand, corresponds to the warrior type, adventurous and with leadership skills, is conscious of power relations and is willing to seize opportunities. Blood group 'AB' is the craftsman, rational, a problem solver, but distant and cold. Blood group 'B' is stated to be possessed by merchants, independent, cheerful, entrepreneurial, work around limitations, not observant of rules and not a team player. It is not difficult to logically match the descriptions for each blood group with job profiles within a company, thus making selection of candidates much easier. All Japanese companies do not subscribe to ketsu-eki-gata, and Count Dracula is not likely to have a job waiting for him with Japanese head hunters (the term head hunters takes on a slightly macabre connotation) anytime soon).

Meanwhile, in another part of the world, the Greeks are hunting the wrong head. Costas Vaxevanis, a Greek journalist has gone on trial for publishing a list of 2,000 Greeks with Swiss bank accounts, and faces a prison term for breaking privacy laws. The Swiss bank accounts are probably being used for tax evasion by high net worth Greeks and the list is being called the 'Lagarde list'. While the authorities in Greece are aggressively pursuing the case against the journalist, no action has been initiated to determine the extent of tax evasion. Jim Boumelha, the president of the international federation of journalists, termed the case against Vaxevanis an 'absurd farce' and has asked for the charges to be dropped. Tax evasion appears to be a lifestyle in Greece that nobody is ready to surrender.

As the race for the US presidential election draws to a close, the attack on private equity has been cranked up several notches. Campaign commercials have painted the role of private equity firms in dark colours, and have compared their behaviour to vampires (proponents of private equity counter this with the 'blood bank' theory), while describing private equity as 'rogue capitalism'. Unfortunately, public equity has not fared particularly well either, and the number of companies listed on US stock exchanges, has declined by over 35 percent since the 1990s. Public equities have yet to resolve the problem relationship between owners and managers. The granting of stock options has not helped to align managers with owners. Public equity markets have come to include the archetypal 'daisy chain', where dealers sell stocks to each other (often times automated) to create a vision of trading volumes, attempting to increase stock prices. The odds are that decades later, the debate between private and public equity will not be resolved by the Gaian hypothesis. Business practices do not evolve quickly enough and business structures are rarely innovative. The selection of investors to provide funding to start-ups as well as mature businesses is yet to evolve sufficiently. Ketsu-eki gata, or selection of investors by blood type is not likely to be a preferred system even in Japan, and blood banks are unlikely to upstage Swiss banks.

Genba Shugi

Innovation is the strategic priority for all business entities. In a recent survey covering more than 400 companies, it was discovered that seven of the top 10 innovator companies were not among the top 10 companies with expenditure on innovation. The list of the world's top 10 innovative companies included, expectedly, Amazon, Apple and Google, however, the 2011 list also included for the first time three Asian companies – Tencent (China), Hindustan Lever (India) and Bharat Heavy Electricals (India). The roads to innovation taken by companies in the 'developed' western world differ significantly from the Asian approach.

Western companies spend huge amounts on innovation and believe, essentially, in serendipity (chance discoveries). The word 'serendipity' itself has strange origins. Sri Lanka, formerly Ceylon, was called Simhaladvipa (island dwelling place of lions) in Sanskrit and Sarandib in Arabic. Horace Walpole coined the word 'serendipity' in 1754, based on the accidental discoveries of heroes in the fairy tale 'The Three Princes of Serendip'.

Vijay Sharma of Hindustan Lever (HLL) and Joichi Ito are among those who practice innovation through Genba Shugi (learning by doing). HLL's Project Shakti is based on Vijay's hands on work with consumer activists and non-governmental organizations. The project has provided training in selling, commercial knowledge and bookkeeping to under privileged rural women, helping to develop thousands of 'micro entrepreneurs'. This innovative network marketing project now covers over 130,000 villages.

As a child when Joichi Ito (one of the world's cyber elite and one of 25 most influential people on the web) wanted to buy a tropical fish, he first took up a job in the pet store and learned how to take care of the fish, cleaning 90 fish tanks every day. When Ito wanted to learn more about the Middle East, he relocated to Dubai. Ito does not have a university degree and is the director of MIT's Media Lab. His interests include dive physiology and industrial music, was angel investor for Twitter, Flickr and is a friend of the founder of LinkedIn. At MIT's Media Lab, students are paid a stipend. Rooms have names that sound like chambers out of a Harry Potter's novel (Mediated Matter, Viral Spaces etc.). The Media Lab generates around 20 patents each year and companies sponsoring the lab have a share in the intellectual property without having to pay any royalties or license fees. Ito's projects seek convergence between design, multimedia, technology and human adaptability.

The serendipity approach that results from the western notion of throwing money at a problem and letting innovation happen, is dying fast. The farmers of Tourteaux Co-operative in France, use transportation powered by bio fuel that uses duck fat and frying oil collected from waste recovery units at restaurants. In the UAE, vegetable oil that has been used at a chain of fast food restaurants is being processed into bio fuel for delivery vehicles. RIM (makers of Blackberry), on the other hand, is shrinking in the face of Apple's iPhone and handsets using Google's Android operating system. The lack of innovation at RIM is hurting, and the innovation premium it once enjoyed is disappearing.

A recent example of creative innovation in business models comes unexpectedly from the apparel sector. J Hilburn in the US (casual wear for men) uses the internet only as a shop window, sends style advisors to visit clients, pays them sales commissions instead of fixed salaries and makes its suits at a factory in Portugal. Missouri's US Congressman Willard Vandiver, would have heartily agreed with Vijay, Ito and Genba Shugi. In an 1899 speech, he famously declared 'you have got to show me'. The un-official state motto of Missouri, to this day, is 'show me' or learning by doing/ seeing.

Getting a Grip

It is finally going to be a lot easier to get a grip on matters, now that the Perfect Handshake (PH) has been encapsulated in a mathematical formula, as a result of the 'Get a Grip' study commissioned by Chevrolet. The PH formula was designed to help Chevrolet sales staff, and is based on factors such as degree of eye contact, completeness of grip, position of hand, strength of grip, dryness of hand and duration.

A French politician (and former synchronized swimmer with little background in economics), was recently appointed as IMF head. The new chief will doubtless, have to draw upon vast experiences as a synchronized swimmer to resolve the financial crises in EU countries. In sharp contrast to the EU, India's PM is a noted economist with virtually no political base, and not surprisingly, India does not find itself in a debt predicament. Meanwhile, German tax payers, perforce getting to grips with the English language, have noted with fear that 'Greece' rhymes with 'fleece' (aka a rip off). In the second phase of the internet boom, e governance, e books, e mail and the like, it fits the pattern that the next largest threat to the global financial markets stems from the debt crises in the 'e-U' and that their most infamous bacterium is now 'e coli'.

Auctions and online auctions have for long been interesting means of trading value. The English auction format (where the highest bidder is the winner) is losing ground to other auction formats, in line with the increasingly more interesting items up for auction. In second-price auctions, the highest bidder wins, paying only the amount of the second highest bid. The Dutch auction format commences with the auctioneer stating a very high price and successively lowering the price until a firm offer to buy is confirmed.

Wayne Sharpe's barter card system, founded in Australia may just be another solution to exchanges values. Barter card supports a trade exchange system that operates in over 12 countries, with nearly a 100,000 barter trading members. Members exchange their own goods and services to pay for what they want. Key benefits include reducing non-moving or less productive assets, reduced transaction costs, increased sales, reduced seasonality of sales, improved cash flows, and expanding the seller's geographic market base.

Getting a grip on the on the amount of outstanding public debt is now a major concern for many countries. The biggest asset sell offs, are therefore, the sale of state assets, as privatization efforts sweep across many countries. Government revenues from such sales exceeded US$ 200 billion in 2010. Mega deals on the table for this year include Poland's mobile phone operator, Mongolia's mining company (30% stake IPO), the US Treasury's shares in General Motor's financial arm, a Russian bank, an energy company and the national airline in Portugal. Greece's privatization plan includes around US$ 70 billion over roughly four years.

Recent auctions have also provided interesting insights on perceived value. A Michael Jackson leather jacket was auctioned for US$ 1.8 million, a photograph of a 19th century American outlaw was sold for US$ 2.3 million and, a former British Prime Minister's handbag fetched US$ 40,000 at a charity auction. On the other hand, Austria's federal real estate company was reported to have considered a rocky proposal of divestment (two peaks all of 1.2 million square meters) for a mere minimum of US$ 170,000. At current values, it would take 12 such peaks to buy one MJ leather jacket or photograph of a 19th century outlaw. It could also imply that roughly four handbags (presumably, and unsurprisingly empty) of an ex British PM are quite adequate to buy two Austrian Alpine peaks !!

Gracias Por La Visita

Impact investing or 'patient capital' involves utilizing profit seeking investments for social and environmental betterment. Mainstream commercial capital is attracted into social sectors such as infrastructure, healthcare, water, integrated technology solutions, affordable housing, primary education, agriculture and micro finance. Social impact bonds ('SIBs') are also perceived to have an important role in developing public services such as sanitation and renewable energy. Impact investing, SIBs and social venture funds are being positioned as a distinct asset class. 'Impact first' investors follow the main objectives of developing the social sectors and willingly accept comparatively lower rates of return on investments. 'Finance first' investors target market comparable returns while supporting social good (as a by-product). JP Morgan recently estimated that impact investing represented an opportunity of around USD 1 trillion over the next ten years, with an estimated profit potential of as high as USD 665 billion. The long term return on equity for impact investments in emerging markets was forecasted to be around 24 percent.

Governments fund infrastructure and environmental investments using impact investing. China is constructing an intermodal, sea-land transport link to Myanmar. The expressway is over 128 kms long, includes nearly a 100 bridges and 15 tunnels. The great green wall ('GGW') project was initiated by the African Union in 2007. A 15 km wide stretch of trees is being planted, over 7,600 kms, across eleven countries (Dakar to Djibouti), to halt the advancing desert. The GGW will help natural water reservoirs, nature reserves and routes used by herds. Botanists and soil specialists have chosen plants that adapt to harsh conditions. A French human environment observatory was also set up in 2009 to study the impact of the reforestation initiative. Plant species that are not attractive to loggers, but yield fruit and oil are being selected. Market gardens on the project produce tomatoes, lettuce, melons and potatoes.

Elsewhere, in South America, a massive highway has been completed. The 'Inter Oceanic Highway' connects Brazil's Atlantic coast with Peru's Pacific ports. The road drives through the Amazon jungle, glacial peaks and then reaches down to Peru's ports. The final stage is the Billinghurst, a bright orange bridge built over the Peruvian river Madre de Dios. A green sign board in Puerto Maldonado reads 'Gracias por la visita – Rio de Janeiro – 4,373 km' – a quiet, modest statement, recording a stupendous achievement. An ambitious Chinese project aims to link, within the next decade, King's Cross in London to Beijing by rail, an 8,000 km journey over just two days, over a high speed rail link, at over 200 miles per hour. Passengers enjoying the experience could make it in another day, to Singapore on an extension of the line, a further distance of 2,680 kms.

Another example are the brown wastes of the Gobi desert in Mongolia that are now home to Turquoise Hill, the site of the largest undeveloped copper and gold mine in the world. Turquoise Hill in the Gobi employs over 15,000 workers and is likely to produce over 400,000 tons of copper each year by 2020. This project would account for over a third of Mongolia's GDP. Mongolia has two neighbours, namely, Russia and China. China buys over 80 percent of Mongolia's exports including coal. The countries with most Mongolian expatriates, however, are South Korea and the USA.

The redoubtable Colonel Sanders once remarked that it served no useful purpose to be the richest man in a cemetery. Steve B, known for The Postman Song, number 1 on Billboard charts in the 1990s, was recently hauled off stage during a performance and arrested for over USD 400,000 in unpaid child support. Unfortunately, Steve clearly, did not have the benefit of Colonel Sander's kindly advice.

H Silent

The recent election of Francois Hollande has brought to the fore, the debate of 'H' silent. H silent stands for the ninety nine percent who have been largely silent for the past two decades – (h)ungry, (h)angry, (h)uro zone, (h)austerity, (h)inflation, growt(h), safe (h)aven, (h)waii,

Its' been years since there was an official study relating the developments surrounding male facial hair and economic or social developments. In prehistoric societies it was common for me to have a beard, however, that was probably because the shaving kit had not yet been invented. In ancient civilizations beards were a sign of honour and were cut only as a severe form of punishment. Alexander the Great insisted that his soldiers could not have beards and the logic of that seemed questionable. 16th century businessmen came up with the ideas of forked and stiletto beards. Bearded men were viewed in western societies as less caring, less cheerful and less generous. Among Celtic tribes Otto the Great swore by his beard when decreeing something serious. President Lincoln made beards popular for Americans, however, only five Presidents wore a beard and only two more had moustaches. Liberty and the economy in the USA seemed to do particularly well under Presidents with facial (h)air. William Howard Taft (1913) was the last President of the USA to sport a moustache and since then national debt levels have risen significantly. The moustache and beard in western economies has been associated with solid blue collar workers and the clean shaven look, in more recent times, in the west, has been associated with the '1%' banking look. Somehow, clean shaven austerity protesters in Europe, do not look as convincing. Of course, it has not helped matters that Steve Jobs did have facial hair and Bill Gates does not, and that is only the thin edge of the wedge between Apple and Microsoft.

John Montagu held several important public posts during his lifetime, including Secretary of State and First Lord of the Admiralty. His lacklustre performance in public service led to the phrase 'seldom has any man held so many offices and accomplished so little'. John Montagu's lasting legacy, however, had little to do with the posts he held with or without distinction. Montagu was the 4th Earl of Sandwich and was known to eat meals in a hurry – slices of meat placed between two slices of bread. His friends ordered 'the same as Sandwich' and the 'sandwich' was born. 2012 may or may not be the last year on the Mayan calendar, but it is the 250th anniversary of the sandwich – a memorable event in human history. Lord Sandwich was also a supporter of Captain Cook. Captain Cook (strangely, almost everything lasting that Montagu accomplished had an association with food) named the Sandwich Islands and Montague Island off Australia, the South Sandwich Islands and the Montague Island off Alaska, after Lord Sandwich. The Sandwich Islands were later renamed Hawaii. The restaurant sector, thankfully, stayed with the 'sandwich', somehow having a 'Hawaii' would not seem the same.

The business of aromas and scents has made huge strides in the past two decades. There is 'Motor Oil' by Save on Scents that captures the thick scent of engine oil, Gasoline, also by Save on Scents that has the scent of octane. Air Aroma out of Australia has created the scent of technology, replicating the scent of a fresh MacBook Pro. Leather Scent, by Chemical guys is a spray that is recommended for cars, boats, hotels, schools, restaurants, and upholstery generally. Patrick McCarthy, a vice president sales at Microsoft is better known for working to create 'Money' which is cologne that smells like new dollar bills. 'Money' after its launch comes in both' his' and 'hers' version, and sells for less than fifty dollars.

Hanny's Voorwerp

Hanny's Voorwerp is a strange object in deep space with a giant hole at the centre, not unlike the credit and food crisis and some equally strange economic and business phenomena nearer earth. People's humble co-operatives have proven more effective in several countries, than governmental intervention in managing both food and credit.

Co-operatives have long been a useful means of productively engaging people, in capitalist, socialist and communist economies alike. Co-operatives are generally characterized by values of self-help, self-responsibility, high ethical standards and democracy. Co-operatives can help with issues such as credit and food security, distribution of wealth, resolution of social unrest and mitigation of the effects of structural and cyclical unemployment. A broad spectrum of business areas such as financial services, housing, insurance, marketing of agricultural and farm products, health care etc. benefit from co-operative intervention.

A co-operative is owned and controlled by the people who use its services, are employed by it or provide the co-operative with goods and services for distribution. The Fenwick Weaver's Society in Scotland in 1761 that sought to provide savings, loans, education and food distribution services to workers was probably the first recorded co-operative initiative. The first co-operative lending institution was established in 1872 in the UK and in 1895 the International Co-operative Alliance

('ICA') was established. ICA today has member organizations from over 85 countries, representing over 800 million individuals. The ICA has regional offices in Europe, Asia Pacific, the Americas etc.

The Co-operative Group in the UK has nearly 2 million economically active members, over 85,000 employees, and annual sales in excess of £9 bn. The Co-operative Group's business interests include food stores, high-street banking, internet banking ('Smile' was the first full internet bank in the UK), insurance, travel, health care (over 400 pharmacies in the UK), legal services etc. Nearer home, The Dubai Co-operative Society in a leading provider of Halal food products in the Middle East with gross sales estimated at around US$ 50m. In the US, co-operatives cover nearly 120m nationals.

In India, the first co-operative societies' Act was passed in India in 1904 and 35 percent of fertilizers, 55 percent of sugar, 60 percent of cotton and over 50 percent of edible oils are distributed in India through co-operatives. 'Amul' formed in 1946, as a dairy (milk, yoghurt, cheese, ice cream etc.) co-operative movement is perhaps the best example of co-operative achievement in the developing world. Amul has over 2.5m producer members and annual sales in excess of US$ 1.2 billion.

Multi-activity co-operatives help creation of new businesses by entrepreneurs and would potentially be especially valuable from the perspective of gainful employment of nationals in the GCC and for the development of the non-oil sector.

Two recent business 'Voorwerp's' include a compensation battle now at an end and a fresh renewable source of energy. At the time Wimbledon' grass court championships were being played out in July, a different 'grass court' victory made the news. Richard Grasso's court victory allows him to hold on to his famed US$ 187.5m pay packet as head of NYSE (1995 to 2003).

Toronto now provides 15% of the city's drinking water, and cooling power to nearly 50 buildings in the city's core financial district through a US$ 200m project that pipes up cold water from the depths of Lake Ontario. The deep water cooling project provides over 60 megawatts of energy. Mother Earth of course has an abundance of this 'cool' resource. Oil currently provides only around 35 percent of the world's primary energy needs and this recent project could just prove that water is thicker (albeit economically) than oil.

Hadron (Sobre Ruedas)

An astonishing experiment was conducted on the Franco-Swiss border. The Hadron Collider was used to crash atoms through a 17 kilometer tunnel. The outcome was uncertain and fringe speculators half expected a massive blast. However, nobody really expected the amazing outcomes in September – the tripping of financial markets, the first US ban on short selling since the 1929 melt down and, the failure of the Hadron Collider tunnel itself leading to its premature shut down. Indeed, all in all, a truly remarkable September, focus quickly shifting from Hadron Collider to Financial Cauldron.

The tripping of the financial markets led to an early Christmas with the US government pushing for a USD 700 billion bailout package. A few startling facts have emerged. Less than 50 million voters in the US and less than 1,000 individuals, decide the fate of financial markets that impact, one way or the other, over 6 billion people. For the first time in living memory, heads of government and central bankers have been working weekends, together, and on a real issue.

In the case of one failed bank, nine of ten external directors were retired individuals. Their post retirement primary pursuits included production of Broadway plays, oversight responsibilities at the American Red Cross and the Girls Scouts. These were not boards that were properly equipped to defend the interests of shareholders or question the course of action taken by executive officers. Apparently, the theory of good corporate governance and risk management is well established, little supported and just about tolerated.

Asset backed lending, the holy grail of naïve bankers worldwide, came in for much, long delayed criticism. The astonishing lack of scrutiny of the capacity to repay debt obligations (in favor or lending based on the value of assets), with little regard to the predictability, complexity and sustainability of future cash flows, exposed a rapidly advancing financial forest fire. Cash has always been king, 'no cash flows – no business' has been the revered mantra of all successful businesses.

Savings and insurance firms weren't supposed to speculate with their assets, others' assets, even non-existent assets. Savings and insurance institutions were supposed to be the back bone of that mythical legend – the 'faceless, humble middle class' consumer, now likely to be the new star of the movie 'I am Legend II'. 'Risk', 'Fair', 'Bond' and 'Save' are definitely not four letter friends that will walk together anymore. 200 years of spread of capitalism and democratic institutions have not proved quite sufficient to empirically challenge the success of other forms of economic and social governance. The increasing disruptions in capitalistic institutions during the past 100 years, brings into question the validity of the fundamental premises of capitalism.

In an age of young blood, early burn outs and quick retirement plans, Warren Buffet and ageing Central Bankers have waded into the financial mine field, pitching in like modern day Florence nightingales, soothing frayed financial nerves. On the other hand, a recent UN summit called for focus on 89 millennium development goals, goals, targets and indicators – none of which included financial market troubles, assuming that these somehow mysteriously resolve themselves.

Banestro a midsized lender in Spain has recently offered customers free cars in exchange for interest free long term deposits. The scheme is called 'Sobre Ruedas' (smooth running), and is considered a 'win-win' barter, for customers and auto manufacturers. An opportunity for banking and automotive shareholder groups to fire up both markets in one go. A remarkable and complete reversal of roles – buyers now finance sellers instead of the other way around. Sobre Ruedas to all of us.

Happiness is the Road

A recent survey by the credit rating agency Experian revealed that a majority of small business owners in the UK had not heard of 'crowd funding'. The typical small business owner turns to their banker or accountant for advice to resolve short term cash flow problems. Only seven percent of those who were polled said they would search the internet. Crowd funding describes efforts via the internet to pool and raise resources. Crowd funding has been used to support disaster relief campaigns, artists, movies, software development, startup companies, journalists and even political campaigns. Perhaps the first instance of crowd funding took place in 1997. Fans of the British rock group Marillion raised US$60,000 for their US tour. Marillion later used this method to fund albums such as 'Marbles' and 'Happiness Is The Road'. Crowd funding investors receive frames of a film, theme music or special edition downloads. Micro patronage is another related term that was popularized by blogger Jason Kottke in 2005. Micro patronage allows many small patrons to donate small amounts. Kottke quit his day job as a web designer in 2005, and graduated to blogging full time, the voluntary contributions (donations) of his readers supporting his efforts.

The Monalisa is on the bank of a river in Paraguay, near the Brazilian border. This Monalisa is a six-storey, air conditioned shopping mall that attracts thousands of Brazilians. The free trade zone in the border region is an oasis for Brazilian shoppers looking for branded shirts, perfumes, champagne and other luxury consumer goods. High street brands are relatively expensive in Brazil. Oscar Freire Street (Brazil's Fifth Avenue) has shops that sell high street brands at nearly four times the prices in New York or London. Taxes can add up to a hundred and thirty percent to the cost of the goods. Prices are also high on account of the smaller size of orders, higher operational costs, poor infrastructure and high interest rates (inventory holding costs).

Another peculiarity of the Brazilian retail market is that consumers buy almost everything on credit. Credit is provided by stores with instalments up to sixty months. Interest rates can be as high as six percent per month and are usually included in the retail price. Consumers in Brazil also tend to equate quality with price and expect foreign luxury brands to be phenomenally expensive. There are few opportunities to shift production to Brazil since the customer base is typically not large enough. Meanwhile, travel agents continue to offer shopping trips to Florida, promising tours that will help Brazilian tourists enjoy the 'marvels of shopping in air conditioned stores'. Hennes & Mauritz (H&M) plans to open its first store in Chile. The new store will be followed by an even bigger store in Mexico. H&M's new target markets will include Bulgaria, Latvia, Mexico, Chile and Indonesia. Cos (a high end brand), Monki (for young women) and & Other Stories (an independent chain of stores) are new focus launches by H&M, together with a major push in online sales.

Brazil has a plan to have a bullet train running between Rio de Janeiro and Sao Paolo. The cost of a ticket on the train would be half the cost of flying and the train journey time would be slightly shorter than the total time involved in using an airline. The country generally lacks basic infrastructure and it could take twice as long to reach the Sao Paolo airport as the flying time itself to Rio de Janeiro. The project is expected to cost around US$ 17 billion (much of the investment in tunnels and bridges), and operators are expected to earn an annual return of around 8 percent above inflation. Happiness is clearly not the road but the rail in Brazil.

Home Alone

The Bank of England (BoE), the central bank of the UK, was established in 1694, and is the world's second oldest central bank (after the central bank of Sweden). This year, the BoE sees a huge break in tradition. The governor of the BoE is usually appointed by the Queen on the recommendation of the Chancellor and the Prime Minister. The appointment is usually from within the bank. The 119th governor was appointed in 2003 and is due to step down in 2013 after two five year terms. For the first time in its 318 year existence, the BoE will advertise for the position of the governor. The Chancellor has stated that key attributes of candidates would be intelligence, independence and integrity. Given that the appointment is usually from within the BoE, the need for an advertisement appears (perhaps unfortunately so) to send out a message that intelligence, independence and integrity are not available within the BoE (at least not for a salary of 300,000 sterling pounds). What is almost certain is that no persons of Greek or Indian (given the current Prime Minister's fear of all things Indian from chicken *tikka* to Indian dance) origin will be considered.

The Indian political system is facing a period of tumult, after the gentle Dr. Singh (India's 13th Prime Minister is an eminent economist) announced a slew of economic reforms. Dr. Singh deemed it necessary to unleash bold policies including foreign direct investment (FDI) in the retail sector, foreign equity participation in the civil aviation sector, disinvestment of select public sector companies etc. The reforms are extremely unpopular with a section of the opposition and threatened to bring down the government. Notwithstanding the threat to his government, Dr. Singh pushes ahead with economic reform. Political leaders in North America and in the Euro Zone, on the other hand, are simply unwilling to take the required steps to recovery. India is known for a high incidence of creative tax evasion (surpassed only by the Greeks). The institutionalization of the retail sector (largely unorganized today) through FDI will help, in the decade ahead, to improve direct and indirect tax collections in the country.

Iceland is another exception. In 2008, Iceland's entire financial system and banking sector collapsed within a week, the currency depreciated by around 40 percent and inflation went sky rocketing. Iceland's fiscal deficit is now just 2 percent of gross domestic product (14 percent in 2008). Bold recovery measures included adopting progressive taxation with greater burdens on high income groups. Fewer cuts in welfare services ensured that the purchasing power of lower income groups was better maintained. Sectors such as tourism, knowledge and high-tech industries were encouraged. Depositors in banks were granted priority over shareholders and owners of bank debt. The developments in India and Iceland only underline the suspicion that the current economic crises is borne out of political and moral deficits rather than fiscal deficits.

Home Depot is Home Alone in China. Home Depot is closing its big box stores in China. Home Depot's retreat is another example of a failure by a western company to transplant a business model to China. Home Depot's do-it-yourself (DIY) format simply did not work in China. The big box stores just did not attract enough customers who are accustomed to shopping at clusters of local stores that offer more choice. Home Depot is closing seven big box stores, losing nearly 850 jobs and taking a $160 million charge. India and China are daunting markets for retailers such as IKEA, Wal-Mart, TESCO and others. The structure of the Asian markets is very different from their western markets and local businesses are extremely competitive in terms of price, availability of choices and service (e.g. anytime home delivery, product maintenance and repairs).

Ichimoku

Ichimoku Kinko Hyo (Ichiumoku) is a technical analysis method that helps to improve the accuracy of forecasts. Ichimoku was developed in the 1930s by a Japanese journalist, Goichi Hosoda. Goichi worked on the method for nearly 30 years and released his findings in the 1960s. Ichimoku known as the one glance equilibrium chart, is a trend identification system that contains more data that standard candlestick charts. The system includes the Tenkan-sen which is an indicator of the market trend and the Kijun-sen that acts as an indicator of future price movement. A unique feature is the Kumo cloud on the chart that changes in shape, height, thickness and angle depending upon price changes. The Kumo cloud provides indicators of market trends such as bullish, bearish, volatility, trend reversals. The 'Ichimoku' has proven, a further 50 years later, to be superior to traditional price charts, particularly good at forecasting and identifying trends, techniques needed more than ever now.

Harley-Davidson (H-D) is implementing technology upgrades at its production facility in Pennsylvania. The technology upgrade has led to a fall in production and a drop in net income. International sales for H-D account for less than eight percent of the company's revenue. New customer segments that H-D targets are women, ethnic minorities and young adults. H-D, founded in 1903, has survived competition from Japanese manufacturers. H-D bikes continue to be defined by customized chopper style designs, the heavy exhaust note, and the heavy weight machines. William Harley was only 24 when H-D was founded with Arthur Davidson in Milwaukee. The first documented appearance of an H-D was in 1904. From a family backyard shed, a Milwaukee yellow cream brick factory to the headquarters at Juneau Avenue, H-D's story has been a continuous path of product innovation and development. H-D supplied 15,000 bikes to the military during World War I, survived the depression of the 1930s and produced over 90,000 bikes for the military during World War II. H-D bikes were produced in Japan by Rikuo from 1929 to 1958. Production in Japan started out with a 1,210 cc engine. It is rumoured that Goichi Hosoda liked Harley-Davidson motorcycles, their powerful designs and engines. H-D's exhaust fumes could have well been the unlikely inspiration for Hosoda's technical analysis, cloud systems of Ichimoku.

A 'golden rice bowl' in China is not an artefact from the Ming dynasty. A Chinese golden rice bowl is a government job. Instead of bureaucrats and employees of government owned companies leaving to join the private sector, the trend in China is the reverse. Civil service jobs in China are perceived as being comfortable, with less work, subsidized housing, free meals and other benefits, apart from access to corruption tainted ill-gotten gains. Civil sector jobs are also insulated from layoffs, and there are currently, on an average, over 90 applicants for each available position. The golden rice bowl ratio, the number of applicants for each position, is a good indicator of the trend in the people's confidence in the Chinese economy, and stability of private sector employment. At the present, despite government assurances, the people of China are not laying their bets on the private sector, and in the private sector there are over 104 jobs for every 100 job applicants.

Sir John Kiszely (Lieutenant General) resigned recently as President of the Royal British Legion, and Sir Trevor Soars (Admiral and former commander-in-chief) of the Royal Navy resigned as consultant to Babcock International. Both men were caught out making claims about their influence with high ranking officials to secure business deals. It appears that the 'strategic business advice' offered by them was influenced by their 'business interests' with arms manufacturers. A set of illicit connections that Nelson would have frowned upon and Hosoda would certainly not have predicted.

Inclusive Economics

The mobile phone is being used in numerous ways, more so in poorer nations who greatly value the technology. In many poor countries at least two thirds of the population has access to mobile phones that function as distributed computers and are leveraged to provide commercial and social services. More people have access to a mobile phone than traditional banking services. In Sri Lanka, the mobile revolution is called 'more than mobile' and in Africa the slogan is 'from ear to hand'. Mobile phones are used to keep abreast of market prices of goods, send in offers, list openings for low skilled jobs, to learn English on line (in Bangladesh) and to verify product codes on pill packages in order to ensure genuineness.

Mobile phone service platforms have resulted in disintermediation for services such as transferring money and selling tickets to sports events. Payments for salaries, utility bills and even donations are made using text messages. Monitoring of activity levels, traffic situations and stock levels can be paid for by rewarding geographically dispersed participants with free airtime. 'Beeping' is used as a free messaging system by street hawkers to allow regular customers to place orders. Mobile phone technology is used as a commercial force multiplier in poor countries. The otherwise socially and commercially excluded who may not have access to Voice of America, CNN or BBC but have direct and inexpensive access to the voice of the poor. 'Ear to hand' has the potential to banish a hand to mouth existence.

Some North Koreans have found an interesting way to raise foreign currency from South Korea. Online gaming is a serious social challenge in South Korea and is also a business opportunity for North Korean programmers. Parental associations in South Korea have asked for night curfews on children playing online computer games, including on mobile phones. In many of the games, players advance to new levels by acquiring equipment, potions and weapons. North Korean programmers devised software that played popular games online and acquired tools valued by other players. Brokers then sell the tools online to actual players who fast track to new levels in the game. Auto programming is a source of hard currency for North Korean programmers. Myanmar on the other hand, has a very different problem with hard currency. The value of the Kyat has risen by over 25 percent in the past one year and the country has slashed export duties to help exporters.

Just as the Big Mac Index and the Hair Cut Index are indicators of comparative purchasing power and real currency values, the Churn Ratio is a useful indicator of the employment position. Instead of monitoring employers' confidence in hiring new workers, the Churn Ratio monitors the health of the economy and market sentiments by assessing the confidence of employees. In an economy that is not expected to fare well, fewer people opt to switch jobs and this leads to a decline in revenue for employment agencies. The Churn Ratio bears a strong correlation with sales of passenger cars, consumer durables and home loans, and in fact is an early warning signal of impending economic difficulties. This ratio is a lead indicator as compared with the Firing Index (aka Burn Ratio, not to be confused with the television action serial 'Burn Notice') that is a lagging indicator. Meanwhile, the average effective mortgage rate in the US (Bureau of Economic Analysis) is down to 5.3 percent on the back of falling Treasury yields. This has led to refinancing opportunities for home owners who can reduce their original borrowing costs. Comparable home loan rates in Asia are closer to 15 percent and 'home alone' is clearly not an option in Asia.

Indovation

Bees are fond of caffeine. A large number of bees drown in dregs of discarded coffee cups around coffee shops. Bees prefer the sugary caffeine left overs to the hard work of gathering nectar. Nearly one billion cups of disposable coffee sold worldwide each year are an unintended potential trap for bees. Research by a university also shows that the bees prefer their coffee in the morning, with most of them making a beeline for their caffeine fix around noon. Meanwhile, the European Food Standards Authority (EFSA), after a three year period of studies, has determined that water cannot prevent dehydration in humans. Bottled water in the EU now has to prove its worth to humans as a healthy drink by complying with stringent labelling requirements. Interestingly, a number of other, more sociable beverages were not subjected to such scrutiny by EFSA.

Juggad Innovation is the Indian way of thinking lean and generating breakthrough solutions. Juggad, also known as Indovation is a product of the socio-economic environment in the sub-continent coupled with scarcity of capital. Portable ultrasound machines, low cost baby warmers, portable plug in hybrid car fuel kits and rice growing systems that reduce the water requirement, are some examples. Juggad does not focus on discovering the next big idea, rather on making the most of the last big idea. Indovation is quite different from Shanzhai (the Chinese practice of rapid imitation). Shanzhai has led to interesting adaptations, a much quoted example being washing machines with larger outlet pipes that are used by farmers to wash sweet potatoes. Indovation is about making technology affordable and accessible to the masses. It is a bit like jazz music or even music without notes to follow – free flowing and self-building. This contrasts with the approach of global corporations that is typically heavily process driven, well-structured and orchestrated.

An interesting and developing beach line occupation is that of CSE – coconut safety engineer. CSEs are employed at tourist resorts. The CSE ensures that coconuts are retrieved from trees before they fall on unsuspecting, slumbering tourists. Speedy climbing of coconut trees, sharp eyesight and the ability to crack open coconuts for guests are key requisites for CSE job seekers. A new occupation in the US is dumpster diving. Dumpster diving is the art of foraging for edible food from garbage dumps. Large volumes of imperfect but edible food are thrown away by consumers, restaurants and shops in America. All this, while soup kitchens, food banks, food stamp programmes and SNAP (supplemental nutrition assistance program) are helping many American families. Food that is safe to eat may have been discarded because it has damaged looks or is near the end of its shelf life. Dumpster diving communities in many towns include students, homeless and poor families. The core values of these communities are often mutual assistance, independence from state sponsored aid programs, and self-sufficiency by reclaiming discarded food. It is ironic that food insecurity is rampant in America, in the midst of abundance.

The world's global net private financial wealth has been estimated by Boston Consulting Group at over USD 120 trillion. Around eleven million individuals each have more than a million dollars of assets, and collectively hold USD 45 trillion of assets. A very significant proportion of wealth is tax free, either managed through tax havens or classified as non-taxable agricultural or farm income. Unsurprising is the global connection between vote banks and tax free income. As with food, the problem is poverty amidst plenty and the inequalities in distribution. The global economies are not in a recession, only the poor are. Similarly, high inflation has a deeper impact on those who cannot postpone their essential spending. This time it is different.

Investor Man

Superman, Batman, Spiderman, Iron Man – with the spread of investment activities across the globe to enthralling regions, it is inevitable that the super hero of the 21st century will be Investor Man. Sri Lanka, Mexico and Japan are three financial markets that offer interesting investment opportunities.

The USA is unlikely, after a series of foot stomping, mudslinging primaries, to have a lady President anytime soon. Sri Lanka, in contrast, had a lady ruler, as far back as 47 BC. Radio Ceylon is the oldest running radio station in Asia, established in the early 1920s soon after broadcasting was launched in Europe. Sri Lanka has the highest per capita income in South Asia, almost twice that of India.

Sri Lanka's trade relations with Egypt date back to 1400 BC. Nearly 8% of the population is of Arab or Middle Eastern origin. The fall of the Kingdom of Kandy in 1815 brought the entire island under British rule. Ceylon achieved independence in 1948 and the name was changed to Sri Lanka in 1972. The country is geographically, strategically placed and served as an important naval base during WW II. The country is a democracy with a population of just over 20m, creditable literacy rate of over 90% (one of the highest among developing nations) and an impressive life expectancy at birth of nearly 75 years.

Sri Lanka's annual GDP real growth rate is relatively stable at around 6%. Exports mainly include tea, spices, textiles, rubber products, fish, and coconut products. Sri Lanka currently has around 8m mobile telephone lines and this offers good scope for additional penetration. The tax structure is more encouraging to investors than neighbouring countries. Conflict zones account for an estimated 8% of Sri Lanka's GDP. Overseas remittances from Sri Lankan nationals are significant and provide critical balance of payment support.

The Colombo Stock Exchange has over 230 listed companies with an average PE of around 10 and PBV of just below 2. Telecom and banking stocks dominate. Large conglomerates with business interests in property development, food, trading, transportation, financial services etc. offer opportunities for private equity investment.

A bridge is said to have existed between India and Sri Lanka till around 1470 AD. This 48km stretch if dredged, as planned by some politicians (opposed by ecologists and religious groups for various reasons), will result in a shipping canal, a mini Suez, which could save ships a 24 hours loop around Sri Lanka.

Mexico plans to invest around US$ 25bn in infrastructure over the next decade. Windfall export revenues (oil prices) and the strengthening of the peso against the US dollar have boosted the economy. Mexico currently has over 10 percent share in US imports. GM, Chrysler, Ford, Nissan and Volkswagen have significant manufacturing operations in Mexico. The development plans include multi railway routes, cargo terminals, new ports, and the ambitious northern ring road, that will slash transportation time between the Gulf and Pacific coasts and provide access from the industrialized north. Mexico currently accounts for an estimated 5 percent of market capitalization of emerging markets.

Japan's Financial Services Agency is expected to make it easier for their financial institutions to become even more involved in Islamic finance. S&P has a Japan 500 Sharia'h index, Daiwa Asset Management has launched an ETF that includes Japan's top 100 Sharia'h compliant companies. Nomura Asset Management and Mitsubishi UFJ are among institutions that are planning to develop relevant products. Even Toyota has plans to raise finance for auto leasing through Islamic bonds. Nearer home, at least one Kuwaiti bank has participated in a large property deal in Tokyo, involving Islamic financing.

Jolly Good Fellows

Youth unemployment is a critical dimension to the economic crises particularly in the Eurozone. Germany's well-established of apprenticeship is likely to gain acceptance in other European countries and in the USA. Economists at Davos cautioned that youth unemployment is an economic time bomb. Robert Zoellick, the president of the World Bank opined that youth unemployment would lead to a generation of scarred people. The UK government launched the Youth Contract incentive program designed to provide nearly 500,000 employment opportunities for young, eligible workers. A new deal for youth being considered in the US includes a mandatory one year commitment for young people who have either completed or dropped out of high school. The program would give youth a basic monthly income and medical coverage. In addition, more governments are considering proposals to offer tax and financial incentives to companies with jobs at risk. These new forms of national service would clearly be far more productive and beneficial than the compulsory military service that previously existed in many countries.

Eduardo Saverin, the co-founder of Facebook, gave up his US citizenship and became a permanent resident of Singapore. More recently, Trafigura, arguably one of the world's largest commodities trading groups, moved its headquarters from Switzerland to Singapore. Singapore won over Trafigura, competing with Shanghai, Hong Kong and Dubai, and Switzerland's status as the world's commodities trading hub took a major dent. BHP Billiton, the world's largest mining company is soon to relocate its core iron ore and coal marketing divisions from Hague to Singapore, later this year. Singapore is quickly emerging as the trading hub for oil, metals and commodities (agricultural and minerals). Singapore's advantages are better tax regime, sound infrastructure, lower operating costs and the large commodities demand in Asia.

'Jolly Good Fellow' is an official job title at Google. Google's JGF, is an author, self-professed thought leader and philanthropist. Apart from greeting visiting dignitaries with his famous grin, Chade-Meng Tan helps Google employees discover inner peace. Chade was employee number 107 and one of Google's earliest engineers. His training course Search Inside Yourself is designed to ensure that the search engine does not burn out human talent within the company. In keeping with his title of Jolly Good Fellow, Chade has spent a good deal of time, unsuccessfully, trying to get the company to stop paying him a salary.

The central banks of Australia, China, India and Brazil are looking at rate cuts, whereas, the prime minister of Canada is looking for a pipeline, to stimulate economic growth. Environmental concerns in the USA have deferred plans for the 1,700 mile oil pipeline that would have delivered oil from Alberta's oil sands to refining facilities in the Gulf of Mexico. Instead, the Canadian prime minister is now supporting a pipeline to the Pacific coast to deliver fuel to Asian markets. Previously designated commercial interests are now national interests and will probably override environmental concerns in Canada. The diversification away from the US markets is supported and part financed by large investments by Chinese firms and China Investment Corporation, the Chinese sovereign wealth fund.

Coinstar's revenue growth during the past three years, averaged over forty percent. Return on assets, operating profit and investment yields are all far ahead of the market. Coinstar operates DVD vending machines at retailers such as Walmart, has a streaming video joint venture with Verizon, and a partnership with Starbucks (coffee vending machines). Iron Mountain is a document storage company with a healthy return on equity and a gross margin of nearly 60 percent. Regulatory changes, digital archiving and electronic vaults, less than 30 percent current outsourcing of document storage, all represent high growth potential factors. What's in a name? The name in some instances at least, does make a Jolly Good Fellow business firm.

Layman Bros' Debt Race

The irony and tragedy of lending for interest is that a failed financial instrument, adversely affects both the lender and the borrower and, therefore, has a multiplier economic impact. A recent movie in the theatres 'Death Race' (not to be confused with driving in the GCC) gives reason to draw a parallel with the global Debt Race to save failing banks. This is clearly not a market for the layman; these are rough waters needing constant vigilance and alert participation. It is also pretty much clear that in more ways than one, many governments are not likely to bail out the quintessential 'Layman'.

The financial markets have changed – this is the asteroid moment for the financial dinosaurs. Banks that are not nimble enough to adapt and innovate new business models are at risk. The strategy of 'holding out' is unlikely to help since what has taken place is a huge change in the environment. A period of consolidation in the financial sector is more than likely. Risk management takes on a whole new meaning as instead of risk ratings, there are some risks that institutions and high net worth individuals will no longer be willing to take – half way risk ratings are likely to be shown the door, 'black and white' risk ratings are definitely 'in'.

The situation offers tremendous opportunities along with the challenge to innovate and manage change. Sectors that will offer enhanced opportunities include commodities (as countries and companies seek to acquire resources for real products), infrastructure projects backed by governments, waste management and water management projects, education (always a big winner, especially since economic recessions have led to higher population growth rates – women's education and vocational job focused training will be profit leaders), healthcare (people never have enough of this – its almost fashionable to have high medical insurance), food (yes, always a winner, people eat when doing well and eat more when depressed – this is also an economic preference theory – junk food sales will move up), environment management projects. These projects will likely attract private sector investment more than others and offer better than market returns. Transportation and logistics (warehousing, airlines, shipping etc.) is in for a long term down turn as the global economy contracts and the scale of ambitious military and civil projects is down sized.

Investment management and performance turnaround specialists will be in huge demand as companies, will seek to squeeze drops of profits (and cash) out of underperforming investments, and assign success fee based mandates to professionals willing to take the risk and commit time and expertise. Government intervention is overnight not only an accepted norm, but welcomed by capitalists turned socialists. The nice part of being a capitalist is that one can always throw of the cloak and revert to being a socialist, since at the core of every capitalist is a loss taking socialist.

Privatization projects will take a back seat, keeping unemployment and inflation numbers down will be the new key challenges. Privatization projects involving steady income streams, such as, power and water management should, however, fare well. Case in point being the privatization project for the Oman Electricity Transmission Company. Sectors that depend upon outsourcing of processes and the search for alternative energy sources will cool down.

A rather stark fact is that the expansion of the global economy over the past two decades, actually led to the very rapid contraction and internal decomposition of national economies. Tax havens will flourish as corporations will seek to escape the tax man at home. Establishing a tax haven will be an exciting new prospect for small economies.

Marshmallows

The governor of the Bank of England Sir Mervyn King is feeling a bit hot under the collar this winter. The Bank of England has recently set out its gloomiest prediction of economic prospects in the UK (much less recovery) since 1997. The governor predicted 'a period of persistently low growth' and the 'unappealing combination of a subdued recovery, with inflation remaining above target for a while'. The UK's economic output is widely expected to remain below that of 2008 until 2015. The economy is expected to contract further in the fourth quarter of 2012 and in the first quarter of 2013. A 'Paycation' refers to the practice of taking a vacation from one's main job to make and additional income doing some freelance work. Given the bleak economic forecasts, there is currently a strong case for Sir Mervyn King to take a paycation. The Bank of England is probably working on plans to cool down the sterling pound, in a last ditch effort to boost exports and economic output.

Christmas bonus awards in the UK are likely to be significantly lower in 2012, than in previous years. The Financial Services Authority (FSA) has advised banks to scale back bonus payments. The 2012 UK bank bonus pool is estimated at only around 35 percent of 2011 and 15 percent of the bonus pool in 2008. The FSA is clearly taking the view that bank management should pay for the culture of misdeeds, fines, penalties, brand damage, manipulated lending rates, and inappropriate insurance or financial products.

Banks and the financial sector have been generally guilty of 'Voodoo Accounting'. Voodoo Accounting refers to a less than conservative set of accounting practices, designed to inflate revenue, under report expenses and over value assets. Big bath accounting (one time write downs to inflate future years' income), and cookie jar accounting (using reserves from good years) are two of the relatively less damaging components of Voodoo Accounting. The reason that this set of accounting practices is called Voodoo Accounting, is that when accepted practices are applied, the 'profits' booked previously disappear like magic. Most investors will not recognize the signs of Voodoo Accounting, simply because they do not want to believe that company managers are making a trade-off between reporting good results presently and in the future. Walter Mischel, a professor at Stanford, in the 1960s designed and carried out the Marshmallow Test. The Marshmallow Test proved that the majority would prefer to consume now, rather than postpone consumption on the promise of higher returns. What is amazing about the Marshmallow Test is that it was conducted with nursery school students from privileged backgrounds as well as from homeless families. Mischel's Marshmallow Test almost perfectly fits the universe of investors. Most investors do not want to recognize that abnormal returns must necessarily be accompanied by abnormal risks, and will seize (and desperately wish to believe great corporate results), ignoring the fact that it may all disappear in a puff of smoke in later financial years' reports.

Manganese Bronze, the leading manufacturer of London's famed black taxi cabs recently put out a product recall as a result of defective components in the steering boxes. Some of the new parts were sourced from China as part of a cost reduction program. Tourists to London, who find their black cabs on unfamiliar routes and running toward unexpected destinations, can now hold harmless cab drivers since the steering box is to blame. Manganese Bronze, in August recognized a nearly four million sterling pound accounting black hole in the latest example of strange accounting practices coming home to roost. The accounting black hole has quickly swallowed the memory of the under bonnet fires and steering box defects. After four years of losses, the company has entered administration.

Metanoia

The ancient Greek word 'metanoia' means a change of life, a whole new way of thinking, a new direction, a change in priorities and commitments and, a deeply personal change to a new way of thinking. This is perhaps the kind of change required by the Greeks to adjust to a new way of life post the financial crises. Along with the falling stock markets, gold prices and real estate values, NASA added to global woes with a falling satellite. Stock market advice now has four categories – 'buy-hold-sell' and the recently added 'holed'. Metanoia is however, taking place in a number of positive ways in many countries.

A State in India has kicked off an ambitious plan costing over USD 2 billion to distribute free laptops to every student in State government run schools and colleges. The plan will cover 7 million students over five years. And just to hedge bets, in case the laptops are not put to productive use, the government will also be distributing free goats and cows. India's youngest village *sarpanch* (usually village elder - a democratically elected head of a village level institution of local self-government), Chavvi Rajawat, also holds an MBA. The jean clad *sarpanch* has secured a tie up for her village with German software giant SAP, to develop an internet and intranet portal for the village. The project will help the village's projects such as the community centre, computerization of land ownership records, water distribution, the village bank and even a cataract surgery project. The technology education lab at the village will help unemployed youth with e-education projects. The jean clad, young village MBA 'elder' who is pushing business and economic development in the village, is also a trained equestrian, equally at home whether driving a tractor or riding horseback.

Airline passengers are likely to experience a more visible metanoiac turning and change in the world's busiest airports. Jason Steffen has designed and tested a faster method for passengers to board aircraft. The Steffen method could save carriers and passengers costly time at terminals and over USD 100 million a year per major carrier. Steffen's seating plan boards passengers according to window, middle or aisle positions, on alternate rows. Passengers are spaced far enough to allow quick storing of baggage in overhead bins. The standard, usual block boarding, back to front and boarding in random order were all proven to be significantly slower boarding systems. 'Bored while boarding' is likely to soon be a thing of the past. All this change is unlikely to affect Willow (a pet calico cat) who left his home in Colorado, and was found five years later in East Manhattan. The animal shelter who chip-collared the cat will send it off on a plane back home to its owners, strapped in to make sure Willow does not go off wandering again looking for frequent flyer miles.

The ABC of 'metanoia' has touched North America. Alta Bicycle Company (ABC) recently won a contract to put up 600 bicycle stations by summer 2012 in Manhattan and Brooklyn. Over ten thousand bikes will be deployed to popularize a cleaner and healthier urban transport system. The bicycle system will be supported by smart phone applications to update users of availability at the stations. Montreal, Canada too has a BIXI (bicycle taxis) system. Bloomberg's Business Week recently included as part of their run up on fads around the world, some odd and rather unexpected fixations in various countries. In Argentina learning to speak Chinese, in China learning to speak Spanish is a fad, planking kids in Australia and New Zealand, lens less glasses in Taiwan, domestic pets in India, 'Narco Polo' shirts in Mexico, and the sitcom industry in Afghanistan.

Mmemogolo

The economist E. F. 'Fritz' Schumacher's *Small is Beautiful (1973)*, is arguably one of the 100 most influential books written since the 20th century. Fritz who developed Buddhist economics, was economic advisor in India, Zambia, Burma and the U.K. Recent studies show that 15 of the top ranked countries for doing business are small size countries with populations of less than 10 million. These include among others, countries such as Luxembourg, Finland, Sweden, Singapore, Hong Kong, Switzerland, New Zealand, Norway, Austria and Belgium. A whole range of the good things in life including Belgian chocolate and Nokia come from these countries, in addition of course to being home to Peter Drucker, Freud, Arnold Schwarzenegger and Roger Federer.

The list of countries with the highest GDP per capita shows a pre dominance of small size countries (15 of the top 19), including Luxembourg, Norway, Kuwait, United Arab Emirates, Singapore, Hong Kong, Switzerland, Austria etc. These are countries with diverse cultural and economic profiles. The one striking common feature is their specialization or dependence on a specific resource or service – a well-defined economic model.

Mmemogolo's (Queen Mother) son is the 36th Kgosi of The Royal Bafokeng Kingdom of South Africa. This nation occupies less than 2,000 sq.kms in South Africa. The Bafokeng kingdom is fortunate to include nearly

75% of the world's known reserves of platinum. In 2006, royalty payments from the mining company were converted into shares in the company. A corporate structure is being imposed on the nation's finances and a Vision 2020 plan is being implemented. The master plan is focused on distributing the wealth, creating a sustainable economy and reducing long term dependence on mineral resources. The Royal Bafokeng Holdings is managed by professional investment bankers and has assets that are estimated at over R32 billion. And yes, if you are a rugby or football fan, The Royal Bafokeng Sports Palace stadium was a venue for the 1995 Rugby World Cup and is one of 10 venues for the World Cup 2010, with a capacity of over 40,000. The Bafokeng have always been enterprising. When land ownership was restricted to Europeans, the Bafokeng employed missionaries to hold land titles in trust.

Luxembourg (2,586 sq.kms - population around 500,000) is the world's second largest investment fund centre (after the US). Hong Kong (1,104 sq.kms - population of around 7 million) is one of the world's leading financial centres. The Hong Kong Stock Exchange is among the top 6 in the world and the economy is characterized by free markets and government non-intervention. Switzerland (41,285 sq.kms – population of around 8 million) is home to large corporations such as Novartis, Roche, ABB, Nestlé, UBS and others. Chemicals, pharmaceuticals, banking and insurance are key sectors. However, the Swiss found a niche in banking and manufacturing precision instruments. Switzerland is also known for the Red Cross, World Trade Organization and of course – Roger Federer!!

Austria (83,872 sq.kms – population of around 8 million) has a well-developed market economy and is known for industry and tourism. Austria has been home to the likes of engineer Ferdinand Porsche, Freud and economist Schumpeter. Austrian émigrés include management guru Peter Drucker and Arnold Schwarzenegger. Belgium's (30,528 sq. kms – population of around 10 million) exports include food products (chocolate and pralines) and finished diamonds.

Each of these countries has found their economic niche, their sustainable competitive advantage. The Mmemogolos of macroeconomics are clearly the smaller countries, focused on leveraging their strengths and developing specialist expertise. Small is beautiful is even more valid today, than 35 years ago when the book was written by Fritz.

Money Sprinklers

Money sprinklers are what every economy needs today. The People's Daily Online ('PDO') of China plans to list at least a quarter of its equity. PDO was founded in 1997 and is the information platform of the People's Daily. The paper is the daily of the central committee of the communist party of China and has a circulation of around four million. The draft prospectus runs to over 300 pages and is stuffed with traditional verbose prose. Proceeds of the equity issue are planned to be used to develop mobile services and other technology upgrades, in order to develop a true news portal, of the people, by the people and for the people. Meanwhile, online novels and short stories are helping shy policemen and workers in China to become prolific authors.

China's prize winning internet author Li is a policeman, who uses the online pen name 'Red Eyes'. Wangluo Wenxue (network literature) is now the pursuit of millions of Chinese. Serialized fiction with daily updates is rampant with readers paying by the chapter, the downside for authors being that a large number of readers merely download the last or latest chapters. Online readers are insatiable and in some instances demand updates twice each day. Internet authors often have to churn out between 80,000 and 100,000 characters in a day. If the online author is late in adding on new chapters, readers have gone ahead and written their own chapters and even story endings. Top stories include those of Red Eyes (a cop with super powers), Nanpai (stories of a daring tomb raider) and Ren Xin (pen name White Feathered Swallow) who has published books that generate over a million clicks each. Wangluo Wenxue connects people's imaginations.

Kodak, Xerox and even Apple are iconic brands that investors do not believe have bright futures. Xerox's share has lost half its value in the past five years with projected revenue growth at only around two percent. The company does not appear to propose the levels of expansion that would interest a following by value minded investors. Apple is another share that trades at an unimpressive price to earnings multiple that is nearly fifteen percent less than comparable companies. Investors do not believe that future returns will be attractive and, the size of Apple means that it cannot be a takeover target. Apple's successful products are also expected to be commoditized, and with nearly a liquid hundred billion dollars on the balance sheet, investors expect that the only direction is down. Copying leads to commoditizing which in turn leads to the eventual sinking of the brand.

The world's top 5 economies by 2050, (as per HSBC) will be China, US, India, Japan and Germany in that specific order. The world's most used language by 2050 is likely to be Chinese. Matters are not going too well for the UK. Scotland (with the key North Sea oil) is likely to push for independence by 2014 (referendum scheduled), encouraged by the UK's own support of South Sudan. Scotland has a gross domestic product of over a hundred billion dollars and has a high per capita income. The economy in the UK shrank (all lines including production, services and retail) in the fourth quarter of 2011 and is likely to show further reductions in the first half of 2012. The only consolation is that forecasts for the EU are much lower. Careers and places of work for graduates are likely to be increasingly focused around Asia and Africa over the next decade. First quarter earnings of cruise operators in Europe could be sixty percent lower after the recent Costa Concordia disaster. Wary tourists are now taking the Poseidon Adventure (1972) and Cruise Control (1997) movies a bit more seriously and cruise bookings are significantly lower.

Muppets & Pikers

Greg Smith, while resigning from Goldman Sachs said that investment bankers referred to their clients as 'muppets'. The state of the services industries generally, is such that clients are looked at in terms of how easy or difficult it is to get their money. Credit card managers call customers who pay their credit card dues on time as 'deadbeats' because the service providers do not earn interest and penalty charges. In the advertising world, clients are 'bobbleheads' if they approve readily of almost anything. Share brokers on Wall Street classify clients as 'marks' (easy to get), 'pawns' (will do anything) and 'pikers' (small fish). Flight attendants call infrequent travellers 'clampetts' and demanding frequent fliers as 'platinum trash'. To a political advisor, a wealthy client running for office is simply known as 'the check book'. Apparently, the service industry is not yet ready to respect the customer and, 'the customer is always right' has been replaced by 'cash is king'.

Dr. Fill finished only 141 out of 600 participants in the recent American Crossword Puzzle Competition. Dr. Fill is an artificial intelligence (AI) computer program. The problem with computers for robots and other AI applications is that computer programs cannot detect humour, and this is apparently a serious working limitation. It is a limitation since most humour is based on a response that is surprisingly different from an orthodox, expected, or patterned response. Unorthodox situations and jokes that a three year old would understand are beyond the capabilities of AI programs. Lawrence Mazlack, a computer science professor is working to develop programs that can detect and even create jokes. This is currently a key weakness in using AI in human work or assistance situations. Comedians are obviously one class of working professionals who are unlikely to be replaced by computers anytime soon. Followers of Star Trek will recollect the otherwise reliable Mr. Spock (of pointed ears) who was perpetually at a loss to understand the earthly humour that Capt. Kirk shared with Scotty and Doc McCoy on the USS Enterprise.

Steve Jobs had to leave Apple in 1985, only to return more than a decade later in a more successful avatar. A number of high profile successful people were fired by their employers, and this should inspire those being fired. Perhaps it is a simple matter of learning the hard way to value what we have. Lee Iaccocoa (Ford), JK Rowling of Harry Potter fame (Amnesty International), Bloomberg (Salomon Brothers). Robert Redford (Standard Oil), Thomas Edison (Western Union), Madonna (Dunkin' Donuts), and Walt Disney (Kansas City Star) are some who thrived after losing their jobs.

Sportspersons know which side of their bread is buttered. Gary Player is one of the most successful players in the history of golf, with 165 tournament victories on six continents. Gary Player who was known as Mr. Fitness and an international ambassador for the sport was recently asked who he would have liked on his all time great team. Without any hesitation, Player

149

replied 'Gandhi, Mother Teresa, Mandela and Evangelist Billy Graham'.

The BRIC nations recently agreed to conduct bilateral trade in their own currencies, and to work toward establishing a development bank that would reflect their needs. Brazil and China have begun talks in earnest to improve bilateral trade between the two countries. China currently, buys few products from Brazil other than commodities and Brazilian exports have faced a downturn on the back of the troubles in the EU and in the USA. In a first step, China has agreed to purchase 300,000 donkeys a year from Brazil. While this is still a long way off from buying industrial products, it is a hoof in the right direction. Not great news for the animals that are probably used to a laid back lifestyle.

Newton's Laws

The recent financial crises have made people review the concept of money itself. Money was invented as a device of convenience. Over time, money has dominated every aspect of human existence and is often confused with wealth and happiness, overriding ethical values and environmental concerns. Counters of wealth (bankers), are rewarded many times more than creators of wealth (skilled technicians, researchers, artists, doctors, farmers, builders, and teachers). Protection of wealth creators is the safety belt that today's societies have abandoned. Most economists are particularly good at explaining the past and universally poor at predicting the future. Immersed in mathematical equations, economists support theory with strings of unrealistic assumptions, ignoring opportunity costs of resources and market reactions. Society and country specifics are usually abandoned in favour of broad brush generalizations.

Sir Isaac Newton, often inaccurately described as a mathematician and physicist was perhaps the first real economist (if not the last), even before Alfred Marshall. Newton's universal laws of gravitation, laws of inertia, mass and acceleration and law of opposite reaction were assumed to apply only to the physical world, whereas Newton was probably one of the first truly great economists. All of Newton's laws of natural physics have been shown to be elemental to the business world. What goes up must come down, what is in motion continues unless acted upon by an unbalanced force (resistance to change), a larger force is needed to accelerate a larger mass (basic macroeconomic stimulus theory), equal and opposite reactions to exertion of force in any direction (basic fiscal and monetary policies).

Global commerce has so far consumed roughly half of the earth's resources of coal, natural gas and crude oil. Survival of societies in the latter half of this century will depend upon successful de-industrialisation. By the third decade, large economies will move to scarcity industrialism, focusing on efficient use of remaining fossil fuels. Scarcity industrialism, by the fourth decade will develop into salvage industrialism based on subsistence technologies, designed to leverage legacy resources. By this time fossil fuel using economies will be in turmoil. Coal and oil will become historical curiosities and eco-technically efficient societies that rely on renewable sources of energy will flourish in the second half of this century. The wasteful abundance of today's societies will be buried in the history books as with the grand Mayan, Egyptian, Greek, Roman and Persian civilizations.

The price of oil is situational. While still underground, oil may sell for the equivalent of USD 35 a barrel, processed through a refinery the price could be well over thrice that amount, once spilt by a tanker into the water, the clean-up costs are massive. An oil spill clean-up can easily cost up to USD 6,000 per barrel (nearly 175 times the cost of the oil). These costs can quickly rise, with legal costs, environmental restoration costs and compensation for lost profits to local industry.

Like spilt milk, spilt oil is bad news, only much more costly. A recent oil spill in Brazil's Campos Basin resulted in a USD 10 billion lawsuit against Chevron. Needless to say, oil spills at the time of an election costs the oil company a much bigger hole in their budget. Meanwhile, everybody's favourite billionaire, Warren Buffet recently recorded a song for a spring festival gala, an entertainment show that has a small matter of a few hundred million viewers on Chinese New Year's eve. Buffet has already done an Axl Rose impression in a Geico ad and appears to have yet another career break up his sleeve. Buffet's Geico ad was good enough to make viewers feel like buying insurance even if they did not have anything particular left to insure, other than their own feelings.

Niue Lessons

The first nation in the world to provide free wireless internet access is Niue. Niue is north east of New Zealand and has around 1,400 residents. All Niueans are citizens of New Zealand. The country is all of 260 square kilometres. The Rock of Polynesia (also called simply 'The Rock', not to be confused with the American actor and wrestler Dwayne Johnson). Niue has an internet users society, is a member of the UNESCO and the WTO. The island country has come a long way since 1774 when Captain Cook named it the Savage Island. The name Niue itself translates as 'behold the coconut'. The government established the Fonuakula Industrial Park to help the private sector. Niue is also known for vanilla plantations and the food chain includes pink taro (a vegetable that looks like a potato), uga (coconut crab or 'robber crab' a crab that can climb but cannot swim), noni (a fruit), and hulahula (red bananas, not to be confused with the hula hoops of ancient Greece).

Meanwhile, hotels and inns in the Caribbean are very concerned about the state of the economy in the US and UK. The sharp reduction in tourist inflows has pushed the level of debt to unprecedented levels. Caribbean nations such as Belize, Jamaica, Barbados, Grenada, Antigua, Dominica and others are struggling under the burden of huge national debts. Spending by running up huge deficits, the demise of their sugar industry, tropical hurricanes, the decline in tourism, the collapse of insurance companies have given rise to imminent national debt restructuring projects. St. Kitts ('kittians') are however, an optimistic lot and are constructing an airport for private jets. Sunny Kittians are betting that there is no real shortage of billionaires (or at least multimillionaires).

The world is getting smaller while the universe is getting bigger all the time. The Hult International Business School awards teams of university students for their solutions to global social challenges. NGO partners of the business school then receive seed funding to help implementation of the winning ideas. One of the winning teams this year was from the Abu Dhabi campus of the New York University. The unusual team (originating from the Middle East) had one student each from China, Pakistan, Taiwan and India. The probability of nationals from these four countries collaborating on any venture, let alone a social challenge project, must be astronomical, whether in a smaller world or an expanding universe.

Nasdaq recently suffered a huge trading glitch and embarrassment. Kraft Foods shifted from the New York Stock Exchange to the Nasdaq. In the first minute of trading, the stock leapt by nearly 30 percent as a result of trades that were processed erroneously (later cancelled). This follows the other high profile glitches of the mishandling of Facebook's public offering and the software error that caused an electronic trading and brokerage company to suffer a US$ 440 million loss. Algorithmic trading at high speeds brings new risks to brokerage firms. The quest for speeds on land continues to test new barriers. A British engineering firm is designing a rocket system that will propel a car at 1,000 miles per hour. The engine, appropriately called 'Bloodhound' was loud enough to break some of the cameras recording the test. The 'engine' is a combination of a rocket and a Formula One engine, and test runs will continue until the team attempts a world record in South African in 2014. This is one engine that will find a ready market with racing enthusiasts in the Middle Eastern countries, especially with the added feature that no speed camera will ever book the Bloodhound with a ticket. Now, all the financial markets need, is an algorithm that trades on the Nasdaq at the Speed of Bloodhound.

Ogopogo & The Funny Fox Trot

A 'cryptid' is a creature whose existence is popularly suspected but has not been credited by scientific evidence and therefore, looked upon as highly unlikely to actually exist. Yeti (Himalayas) and the Loch Ness Monster (Scotland) are examples. The Ogopogo is a unique cryptid. The Ogopogo (also known traditionally as a Naitaka) is a humped lake (sea) serpent reported to reside in the Okanagan Lake in Canada. The name Ogopogo originates from the 1924 music hall song 'The Ogopogo: The Funny Fox Trot' by Clark and Strong. Balancing the budget has now become an Ogopogo cryptid – everybody believes having seen a balanced governmental budget in their life time, but nobody has actual proof of one. Balancing expectations on inflation, currency values, employment and fair trade now resembles the funny fox trot.

All the 2012 Republican presidential hopefuls are millionaires. Prokhorov, one of Russia's presidential candidates is a billionaire several times over. Prokhorov's wealth is estimated at $20 billion and his possessions include a 200 foot yacht, a mansion outside Moscow, shares in a gold mine (literally), and the New York Nets (Prokhorov was the first overseas owner of an NBA franchise). Sections of the electorate believe (or wish) that since he is already wealthy, he does not need to make more money and therefore will be honest in public life (and service). His opponents like him because as an ostentatiously rich individual, he is considered fundamentally unelectable (probably the very reason why he was allowed in as a candidate). His campaign slogan is 'demand more' and focuses on people's dissatisfaction with corruption, restriction of freedom and a general lack of transparency in public life. Sections of the electorate are also firm believers that on a national scale, he could replicate much of the financial and economic success he achieved in personal life. There have been reported sightings of businessmen making Ogopogo-like forays into public life and politics, however, never before has there been such an open run as this. It is a sign of the times that it is suddenly no longer embarrassing to be rich and be paying low rates of income taxes – in fact in times of recession, the super wealthy are increasingly being applauded for their success and their wealth is proof of competency.

Stranger yet are some categories of occupations gaining ground. Setting fire to houses is now a paying job in Australia. Fire scientists study how to make buildings and homes fire resistant. Government research bodies carry out experiments to survey how materials and designs react to bushfires. Systems and tools that help to predict the spread and level of risk from bushfires are developed. Products such as spray defense systems can help protect both lives and property. Toy makers are employing child psychologists to design and develop toys that meet developmental needs and retain interest. Building value into the design is a complex process since it includes play value for the users (children) and perceived value for the buyers (parents). Product design combines the knowledge of child psychology, commercial astuteness and anthropology. Unfortunately, there is an eerie similarity with the methods employed decades earlier by fast food chains and cigarette companies.

Leaping around takes different shapes in various countries. In Hong Kong, persons born on 29 February are given the legal date of birth of 1st March. In China, the legal date of birth assigned is 28th February. February 29 is considered especially lucky for Christopher Columbus and by extension for America. In Scotland, Finland and Denmark women can propose to men on 29 February. Of course it gets quite complicated if a Scottish woman, born in Hong Kong proposes to a Chinese man on February 29th and the couple later has twins on the 28th of February.

Pasty Times

Britain's recent budget included a tax on hot takeaway food. Hot food from bakeries and supermarkets are likely to lose the exemption from the twenty percent value added tax on sales. The tax was quickly dubbed the 'pasty' tax, after the popular pastry from Cornwall. The relatively low cost pasty and its brethren the sausage rolls are consumed heartily by customers feeling the pinch of the recession. It did not help matters that the chancellor, having introduced the tax could not recollect his last purchase of a pasty and the prime minister probably bought one more than five years back. The pasty tax has given a fillip to the opposition party in the UK and underlined the difference between what people at the two ends of the income scale eat in the UK. Marks and Spencer has the credit of carrying an appeal over the rate of taxes on teacakes for over ten years and, 'Pastygate' is likely to run for a while. Hunger Games, meanwhile shows promise of developing into an extremely profitable film franchise. The film has grossed record returns for Lions Gate Entertainment and JP Morgan estimates that the series could deliver profits of over one billion dollars.

Matson and Elliott Handler founded the toy company Mattel in 1945. Ruth Handler (Elliott's wife) later established the Barbie doll product line in 1959. Mattel Inc. produces Barbie dolls, Hot Wheels, Matchbox toys, Masters of the Universe and board games among many other toys and games product lines. Mattel makes products that parents feel compelled to buy even when on a tight budget and, Mattel in short is recession proof. Gross margins at Mattel are almost fifty percent and overheads are controlled. In the past five years since 2007, Mattel shares have returned a phenomenal 84 percent. Parents, while buying Mattel toys, should probably buy Mattel shares for the college fund, as well, or maybe instead.

Another company with exceptional survival skills is Johnson & Johnson ('J&J'). Johnson & Johnson has been around since 1886 with a diversified product mix that includes medications, consumer products, orthopaedic devices and iconic brands such as Band – Aid, Tylenol, Neutrogena, Benadryl, Listerine and baby products. Johnson & Johnson recently made news after the disclosure that the outgoing chief executive officer will be given a retirement compensation package of around $ 140 million. In the ten years that William Weldon led Johnson & Johnson, revenue grew from $36 billion to $ 65 billion a year and cash flows more than doubled. J&J is simply recession proof with a product portfolio that has proven to be ideally defensive through turbulent financial markets.

Peer to Peer ('P2P') lending is growing around the world, in the US, China, UK, India, Germany and other countries. P2P lending has gained impetus as banks and even venture capitalists are increasingly risk averse. Individuals and entities with cash are, on the other hand seeking better returns from investments that are graded by traditional lenders as risky. Some P2P outfits sometimes offer funding participants up to eight times more than the usual bank deposit rates. Social lending is a product of the internet platforms and popular P2P companies are Funding Circle, RateSetter and Zopa (UK), Prosper and Zidisha (US), P2P Financial (Canada). P2P loans have funded small businesses, mortgage payments, student loans, and consolidation of existing debts. Social lending could be direct or pooled, secure or unsecured, and services offered include loan origination and servicing (documentation, payment schedules, collections, fund transfers etc.). The problem of default is covered by a quasi insurance scheme – some firms require each borrower to contribute regularly to a default provision fund, intended to compensate lenders when borrowers default. Social lending based on inter personal networking is working to fill the cracks in a broken financial system.

Peas and 3Cs

The 44th US President recently urged fellow Americans to 'eat their peas', at a press conference, while declaring that he would not accept stop gap measures with regard to the US government's debt ceiling. The US Dry Pea & Lentil Council was of course thrilled at the unexpected and exalted product promotion. Some Tea Party movement supporters quickly pointed out that the US President was finally taking a leaf out of their book (cup) and going green. Democrats however, did not appear keen on being known henceforth, as the Pea Party. The First Lady, then compensated the foot in the mouth episode, with a 1,556 calorie cheeseburger lunch (fries and chocolate shake to accompany), to the extreme embarrassment of her Let's Move healthy lifestyle troopers. The French of course were delighted at the strong note of resonance from the US of A. In more difficult times (the 1775 bread shortage 'Flour Wars' of France), Marie Antoinette, (described coincidentally at the time as 'Madame Deficit'), was attributed the infamous quote (translated) 'if they don't have bread let them eat brioche' (rich, expensive, yellow, egg buns – i.e. cake). Well, it is a bit of an all round come down (236 years notwithstanding) from cake to peas and all parties involved can justifiably feel aggrieved.

History has a nasty way of repeating itself. Popular legend claimed that the Roman Emperor Nero, was rightly or wrongly, considered the Emperor who played the fiddle while Rome was ravaged in the Great Fire of

Rome (July, AD 64). Nero was also the first to devalue Roman currency during the empire's history and, did so mainly to increase public spending on grandiose projects. Fast forward to 2011 – North America and Europe are busy maintaining and preparing skating rinks, while their corporate and government ratings sink. Rating agencies have long since ceased to provide financial markets with early warning signals. During the past two decades, rating agencies have morphed from being purveyors of early warning signals, to tombstones, to working as below the ground post mortem specialists.

The business leadership landscape too is undergoing an interesting change. Hierarchical leadership with a single CEO is considered to be an anachronism. The model of flat leadership with multiple leaders (groups of at least 4-5) is fast catching on. There will be no single team captain. Ideas and values will lead, not individuals. Flat leadership is intended to be inclusive and elevating. Michelle Doyle, Mark Smith and Ric Charlesworth (field hockey legend) have significantly advanced Joel Kurtzman's 1994 concept of 'thought leaders', revolutionizing the very basis of leadership.

Chinese philosophers subscribed to the notion of 'tianxia' (all under heaven – a unified world/ kingdom dominated by one country). Tianxia is a utopian vision of harmony. The business world certainly seems headed there. Anshu Jain, of Indian descent, a London based investment banker, was/ is slated to be the banks' chief executive – Jain, however, does not know the German language and, that is probably the reason why Deutsche Bank has reportedly opted for two co-chief executives (with at least one speaking fluent German). At last reports, Mr. Jain is frantically trying to learn German. Vikram Pandit and Indra Nooyi, Indian born executives who are global CEOs of Citigroup and PepsiCo, must certainly be thankful for their prior knowledge of the English language. The co- CEO model is yet another example of flat leadership in today's business world. . Meanwhile, a growing number of Chinese businessmen strive to learn Hindi, and are based in India. Apart from their fascination with the 3Cs (colors, cinema and curry), the prime reason is their fervent desire to be part of the Indian growth story in the power, infrastructure, chemicals and metals sectors.

Pies and CARBs in the Skies

American Airlines has filed for bankruptcy, in the face of unsustainable payroll costs and rising fuel bills. Every major airline in the US has filed for bankruptcy protection. Cost cutting measures by airlines have proven to be insufficient in America, as in Australia with Qantas. Elsewhere, in India, domestic airlines have approached the government for concessions and support in the face of mounting losses. Domestic airlines in India protested the low fares of the national carrier (support from the government) and the limitations in place on foreign equity participation. Economists are debating, whether any airline operating model can ever deliver long term positive returns to shareholders. Airlines are perhaps best owned and micro managed by employee stakeholders (pilots and flying crews) with smaller airlines feeding into routes managed across regional hub and spoke networks.

Global air freight traffic, once a key profit component of international airlines, continues to drop year on year. Airlines are also one of the most visible polluters. However, it is cargo ships carrying the majority of world trade that use heavily polluting bunker fuel oils. Out of sight is out of mind and their pollution attracts little attention. Cargo vessels have few energy efficiency and pollution standards and are significant contributors to global warming. The basic transportation modes have not changed during the past hundred years, after the initial breakthroughs. Boeing's Dreamliner with huge development costs, is finally in the skies, notwithstanding a landing gear deployment failure during an initial flight. Boeing's programme accounting based the selling prices on a block size order of 1,000 aircraft. At an average selling price of around USD 120 million, Boeing will need cost reduction and efficiency increases, in order to break even on the first block of 1,000 deliveries. The Dreamliner is great news for airlines and passengers, not so good for investors in Boeing stock.

Meanwhile, developers in India continue to dramatically reduce product costs. The Nano, the world's cheapest car in its category at USD 2,500, was followed by Aakash, the world's cheapest tablet (slated to appear across the country in schools and colleges) at just USD 35, has now been trumped by Adidas launching a pair of one dollar shoes. The Indian economy and markets are fuelled by a large and growing middle class population. India faces demand push inflation as disposal incomes increase and supply side and infrastructure bottlenecks continue.

China on the other hand, is experiencing a cooling down in its export driven economy. Domestic consumption in China is unlikely to be able to replace export shortfalls, since disposal incomes are unevenly distributed. Any measures to stimulate the economy in China, therefore, merely result in sharp increases in real estate prices and consumer inflation. Access to and ownership of commodities does provide some countries with sovereign economic security. A major proportion of key global commodities are produced by CARB countries, namely Canada (oil and gas), Australia (iron ore and coal), Russia (oil and gas) and Brazil (iron ore). CARB countries control commodity assets valued at over USD 60 trillion. Columbite tantalite ('coltan') is a mineral that promises to make the Congo wealthy. Coltan is vital to consumer electronic products such as mobile phones, computers and video games and is a critical input to companies such as Nokia, Ericsson, Intel and Sony.

The British Economist E F Schumacher (EF) opined that inventors could not run business firms capably and would allocate resources to endless streams of inefficient innovations. EF would obviously not have seen eye to eye with persons such as Steve Jobs and Sabeer Bhatia (Hotmail and Jaxtr SMS). Innovators have a preference for disruptive technology, whereas financial markets have a preference for steady state technology.

Profits at 12 o'clock

With the price of gold where it is currently, 'all that glitters is not gold' is a heavily underlined proverb for investors in bonds and equities. If necessity is the mother of innovation, recession is the mother of imitation. Imitation has always been a lead indicator of a forthcoming recession. Google's business model was based on that of a company called Overture, a Southern Californian search specialist company. The business model for online search combined display of objective links with paid links. Peter Drucker once described IBM as the world's best imitator for taking concepts from Apple and Commodore machines. Facebook has been accused of copying the idea of a social networking site. White Castle (ten cent slider burgers), who few remember, started the fast food chain concept with standardized store design and operating processes. Diner's Club issued the first credit card, not the now ubiquitous Visa or Master cards.

China has taken the imitation mantra to new levels. 'Varyag', a 1980-90s Russian multi role aircraft carrier was initially purchased in 1998 by Chong Lot Travel Agency. The declared purpose of purchase was to set up a floating entertainment centre and casino in Macau. A few days ago, Varyag set sea on trials as a Chinese aircraft carrier and forerunner of a full-fledged deep sea carrier battle group. Fake Apple stores in Kunming are alarmingly similar to the real stores and even some employees were convinced that they were working for Apple. Ikea's blue and yellow flat packed home furniture model and Subway's sandwiches are two other examples of cloned concepts in China. Pablo Picasso would have approved, the great man once said 'good artists copy, great artists steal'.

Strip malls in the USA are experiencing a happy mushrooming of hair salons. The number of hairstylists and beauty salons in Washington alone has recently grown by 18 percent. Hair salons owners and employees include people turned out and down of other jobs. A significant number of hair stylists have been to college, some with a master's degree. Perhaps the explanation is simple, and in a hair raising economic slump, people prefer to keep it short. The business is inherently defensive in nature since hair salons do not have to worry about clients going to China for a cheaper haircut.

S2S or P2P lending is growing in Asian economies. Strangers or peers borrow from each other small amounts for small businesses, at fixed interest rates for short terms. Lenders benefit through better average returns and low default rates by small businesses. Borrowers with little collateral have access to finance that banks would not provide. The cost of eating out for a family in a big city can sometimes be enough to change the life of a rural family. P2P lending is accessible through web sites to white collar employees.

Not all is lost however, on the innovation front. Scientists in Taiwan have developed a US$2 rewritable electronic paper that can be used without electricity and can be re written up to 250 times. Commercial production is expected within two years. Taste of Darkness ('ToD') is the name of a restaurant in Hyderabad, India. In pitch darkness, guests hold the hand of the visually impaired guide and find their way to a table. ToD offers a four course meal in darkness, giving guests the opportunity to discover food through touch, taste buds and aromas. The menu (Indian and Chinese) is not disclosed in advance to guests. On the tables, water is placed at 11 o'clock and napkins at 3 o'clock– blinded investors are probably hoping that equity gains are at 12 o'clock. After all, a panic is never more than an inch away from a picnic.

Qualitative Easing

The famous (now infamous) Barbary Macaque wild monkeys of Gibraltar are starting to bite people. Gibraltar was a key base for the British Royal Navy and the popular superstition is that if the monkeys leave Gibraltar, Gibraltar will cease to be British. In 1944, the then Prime Minister Winston Churchill sent out a concerned message about the dwindling population of the monkeys, advising the importation of more monkeys, for fear of losing Gibraltar. The presence of the rare monkeys became synonymous with British sovereignty. During the war and in the late 1960s, special attention was devoted to increasing the population of the monkeys. As the monkeys bite back, this is in fact the first known failure of British quantitative easing.

The governor of the Bank of England, who is responsible for the UK's financial system, is required to have an advanced understanding of the financial markets and economic knowledge. The new governor of the UK's central bank is a Canadian. After a process that included an advertisement, one of the most important positions in the stewardship of the UK economy was awarded to a Canadian. The process and the appointment said a lot for the direction in which the UK's financial system and economy is heading. Charlie Bean continues to be the deputy governor. Charlie Bean (no relative of Mr. Bean) is known for his unhappy advocacy of reduction in the levels of household savings in the UK. Quantitative easing never did work and maybe a Canadian will see the Gibraltar episode a bit differently.

Liu Qianping is a seventy two year old Chinese who is also known as 'MaDiGaGa'. Liu who used to be a skinny old farmer is now a supermodel for ladies' wear. Despite having no prior experience, Liu helped increase the sales of the fashion store he models for, by seven hundred percent and there have been more than ten million searches on online social networking sites for MaDiGaGa. Liu who enjoys modelling views his stint as a model, as a temporary shift of occupation and intends to return to his province. An inspiring story indeed, for ageing (or young) unemployed bankers, especially those who are thin, and little wonder that China is not overly troubled by unrest from the unemployed.

One of the oldest surviving monopolies globally is the central banks' monopoly over money. Bernard von NotHaus made a failed attempt to break the Federal Reserve's monopoly in the USA. NotHaus was the creator of the Liberty Dollar, co-founder of the Royal Hawaiian Mint and founder of the Free Marijuana Church of Honolulu. NotHaus was also the founder of an organization (Liberty Services) for the repeal of the Federal Reserve and the Internal Revenue Code. The Liberty Dollar was intended to compete with the United States Dollar. The Liberty Dollar ('ALD') included metal coins, certificates of gold and silver and electronic currency. There were eventually around two hundred and fifty thousand holders of ALD certificates. The circulation of ALD was deemed to be a Federal crime, and nearly two tons of coins featuring the image of Ron Paul (a congressman) were seized, along with gold and silver. In 2011, Bernard von NotHaus was labelled as a domestic terrorist, for his efforts to break the monopoly over money in the United States. These misadventures apart, the United States is a long way off from joining Andorra and Monaco as a country without a central bank, the Federal Reserve is unlikely to hire a Canadian as chairman and Liu Qianping's next job is unlikely to be as governor of the Bank of England or as Chairman of the Federal Reserve. Andorra, bordered by Spain and France, can hardly be faulted for not joining the European Union and for not having a central bank.

Real Steel

This year's scariest costumes for Halloween were European central banker, economist, and Greek politician, closely followed by weather forecaster. Central bankers all over Europe are working weekends to resolve the debt contagion. Belarus is a small land locked country in Eastern Europe, with Russia, Ukraine, Latvia, Poland and Lithuania as its neighbours. The country is looking forward to a relatively minor USD 7 billion bailout from the IMF. Recently, the Belarus' central bank made news for selling off office equipment, furniture and office odds and ends. The sale included over 500 items including paper bags, safes, suitcases, a sugar bowl, a cardboard box, a Dictaphone, an old television set and tapestry. Inflation in Belarus is over 30 percent and the value of the currency has fallen sharply. The list of items put on sale did not include the coffee maker.

The definition of real business keeps evolving. Groupon, launched in 2008, offers daily deals on what to do, see, eat and buy in 45 countries. The Groupon mascot is a chubby cat with a gold necklace. Andrew Mason, the 30 year old founder CEO admits ignorance of financial principles and plans to stay so. But then, financial astuteness is not critical if at 30 you have a company that is valued at over USD 12 billion, employs nearly 10,000 people and has quarterly net revenue over USD 400 million. Technology start ups are following a model of small initial public offerings to support the share price (LinkedIn too sold off less than 10 percent of its total stock). Recent world population studies show that the median age of the world population is 29 and over 70 percent yet do not have access to the internet. Internet start-ups do have a bright future at the stock markets. Zynga, Facebook, Groupon, LinkedIn, together with workhorses Apple and Amazon are leading a comeback on the stock markets for smart and innovative technology businesses.

Brick and mortar businesses have selectively delivered consistently solid shareholder returns in difficult times, if pizza and adhesive can be called brick and mortar. Domino's Pizza's stock price has moved up by over 200 percent since 2009 after the company kicked off an honest advertising campaign that accepted and worked with its reputation for a low cost product. 3M recently dropped its growth target to only around 4 percent. 3M, however, can have single digit growth and still have not too unhappy shareholders. The company's management maintains a steady financial strategy, by closely monitoring cash flows, margins and returns to shareholders (dividends and buy backs), while consistently ploughing back cash into new product development.

Floods in Thailand are likely to push up prices for personal computers and a large number of smaller technology component supplies. Companies that are affected include Acer, Lenovo, Samsung, Toyota, Honda and Nikon. Nearly 30 percent of global hard drive assembly facilities are located in Thailand. The global technology supply chain for hard drives usually has two months of inventory at any point in time. If component suppliers are unable to shift production to factories in other countries, within the next two months, there will be an acute shortage of critical components. While some new product launches are likely to be delayed, hard drive assembly is likely to be seriously impacted since Western Digital, the world's largest hard drive maker was forced to close all its facilities in Thailand. Woes of Sony's shareholders are seemingly never ending. Sony has faced up to a tsunami, loss of a factory in the London riots, a strengthening Japanese yen and the recent floods in Thailand. Sony, however, remains cash rich and has recently committed over USD 1 billion to buy out Swedish partner Ericsson.

Shopping Around

The Chinese are buying up real estate all over the world. For many Americans, the prospect of the dollar not being the global currency by 2020 is far less scary than the prospect that Hollywood could be renamed 'Chinawood' by 2020. In the UK, retail shopping and investments are undergoing significant change. Primary issues of retail bonds in the UK for 2012 are expected to touch sterling 5 billion over thrice the amount raised in 2011. Retail bonds in the UK are attractive to investors seeking higher yields than deposits or blue chip equity shares. A recent trend is to issue retail bonds with a coupon linked to the retail price index. Companies are turning to retail bonds to reduce their borrowing costs. Meanwhile, a large number of small to medium manufacturers in the UK have faced shrinkage of their bank credit facilities, reduction in repayment periods and a rise in borrowing costs. Banks are also shifting facilities of small manufacturers to invoice discounting. The difficulty with invoice financing is that it is linked to specific orders. Product development and capacity building are not financed by invoice financing, which will only serve to accentuate the slowdown.

Shopping trends in the UK show shifts from high streets to out of town retail parks. Out of town shopping has had a damaging effect in terms of spreading around traffic, pollution and on the high street networks. Recent government proposals in the UK will make it harder to set up out of town stores, with the right to veto out of town retail developments. Convenience, however, can hardly be legislated. Shoppers will move for amenities, parking and clusters of a wide retail mix. The protection of high streets and disfavour to out of town shopping centres is another example of politically led economic decisions even in times of recession, which will only lead to further economic constriction.

KIIDs in the EU have too much technical jargon. Ninety seven percent of Key Investor Information Documents (KIIDs) in the EU use jargon and technical terms. A recent survey covered asset managers in eight EU countries and discovered that most KIIDs do not present information in a form that helps investors to understand the content. Most KIIDs convert simple issues to complex jargon in product information sheets. Asset managers counter that examples of plain language have not been provided to them. The font size, size of paragraphs, inconsistency between the investment objectives and risk profile, layout of the document all contribute to KIIDs in the EU that are not investor friendly.

Meanwhile the first even triple A bond default of 2012 (reportedly covered in less than six hours), took place, unexpectedly so, not in Greece or elsewhere in the EU or Americas, but in China. China also experienced the first default on a bond designed for small businesses. Bonds, representing largely shorter term finance facilities, were used to invest in capacity, which has now turned out to be a longer term investment recovery proposition. The bundling up of debt issues of small and medium companies, into a single bond was a

Chinese regulator's innovation to spread risks. Instead, this has resulted in a concentration of credit risk.

The American comic Louis CK distributed his latest piece, online, by himself, breaking the rules of the entertainment distribution channels, and revenues were quickly over a million dollars. Artists with a large following, could follow his example (each download was priced at just five dollars), without having to rely on the distribution skills of traditional channels. The website that CK used, cost only $32,000 to set up and was capable of handling large downloads. Production houses and media that otherwise invest large amounts into distribution infrastructure worry that entertainers with established followings, would now reach fans directly.

Silly Con BRICQ Times

Despite the global financial turmoil, nothing much has in fact changed. The global economy has integrated and moved, over the past 100 years from an Industrial Revolution to a Silicon Valley (Information Technology) revolution, to the more recent Silly Con Wailing (Financial) revolution. In times of wide spread unemployment, new and innovative occupations continue to break ground. Max Durovic is a sign spinner. A sign spinner performs acrobatics and dances with advertising signs, attracting public attention. Sign spinners are giving a boost to the A board (sandwich boards) holders, also known as 'human directional's'. Holding still and pointing are likely to be supplements by more enterprising ways of street walk and plaza advertising. In areas where carrying boards in not permitted, 'human directional's' wear jackets with bright or even luminous arrows printed on the jackets.

Loan officers with a bank in ten African countries are going to use psychometric tests to determine whether entrepreneurial applicants are eligible to borrow and are good risks. It would be interesting if this practice were to develop further and apply even to purchases of government bonds, for example, psychometric testing could be applied to determine whether Greece, Spain or Italy and their people are worth the bailout effort. Employing psychoanalysts as loan officers is an interesting variation on the strong arm loan recovery methods that some lenders utilize. Also, interesting would be if psychometric testing is applied as a prerequisite to other aspects of contractual business dealings.

Russian equities were dumped in recent months, in the general flight to safety. Foreign investors exited in a rush, dropping equity prices by almost thirty percent, whereas usually, Russian share prices closely follow the price of oil. The demand for oil and gas, Russian exports and public finances are looking stable. Putin is likely to safely return to the presidency and provide political stability. The average price to earnings multiple of Russian equity shares is only 6 and this is extraordinarily low considering the stable outlook.

Recent population studies show that 20 percent of the world's population lives in China and its 85 million individual investors will soon be able to buy shares of foreign companies on the Shanghai Stock Exchange. Foreign companies will be allowed to list in one of the world's biggest equity markets. Benefits to companies include higher valuations and access to Chinese funding for expansion on the mainland. Enter the Dragon on the global stock markets will give a fillip to internet and dot com valuations. BRIC (economic bloc) is likely to be spelt in future as BRICQ with the prospective addition of Qatar. The odds are in favour of future major sporting events, even Bond movies being held or based within BRICQs.

Former aid recipient countries are now turning donors. The UK's Department for International Development is phasing out aid to fifteen countries such as Vietnam, Cambodia, Bosnia, Cameroon, Niger, Angola, Burundi, Indonesia, Iraq and Serbia. Meanwhile, there is pressure on Brazil, Russia, India, China and Qatar (BRICQ) to become donors to global funds. Formerly developing countries now have large middle class populations while western economies are floundering, decoupling and deleveraging as the structure of the post 1950s global financial system crumbles.

A researcher at a major university's program in ethics and health concluded after extensive studies that humans are indeed capable of distinguishing between duck liver delicacy and dog food. Another research paper, at another major university, covered thirty seven years of time series data of egg production and chicken population, to conclude that the egg did come before the chicken. It is no surprise, therefore, that serious research supporting advances in medical science makes comparatively little headway and vital medicines take decades to develop.

Humpty SPAC

Humpty Dumpty sat on a private equity wall. Humpty Dumpty had a big fall, and all the world's investment bankers could not make Humpty Dumpty well again - - then came SPACs to the rescue. In early 2008, both NASDAQ and NYSE applied to allow listing of SPACs. Special Purpose Acquisition Companies ('SPACs') are shell companies that are formed with the objective of acquiring an operating company in a specified industry or region. The target operating company is identified after formation of the SPAC. The SPAC first raises funds and then looks for a private operating company to acquire, while at least 90% of the IPO proceeds are put into a Trust account.

A SPAC is a reversible, relatively liquid, shorter term financial commitment. Investors have the right to reject the proposed acquisition. Shareholders who do not approve the acquisition transaction have the right to receive their pro rata share of the balance in the Trust account, including the after tax interest on the Trust balance. Alternatively, shareholders who do not approve the transaction may also sell their shares, since SPACs are liquid and traded. If more than 30% of shareholders reject the transaction, all shareholders receive their pro rata portion of the Trust assets, and the Trust is liquidated. In a liquidation scenario, the Sponsor, usually, loses all its capital (the Sponsor-management team invests 3% to 5% of the SPAC). If the SPAC management team does not succeed in closing a transaction (signing a letter of intent within 18 months) in 24 months (up to 36 months for transactions in countries where closure could take longer), shareholders are entitled to the pro rata distribution of Trust assets.

The Trustee can only release the funds upon receiving the required shareholder approval and the proposed transaction should have a value of at least 80% of the SPAC's net assets. The sponsor-management team is not paid any salaries or finders fees and is usually awarded 20% of the post acquisition common equity. Sponsor's shares are also typically held in escrow for three years, at least one year post closing of the acquisition transaction. After the transaction, the target name is retained and the company registers to trade on NASDAQ or NYSE.

In 2007, an estimated 25% of all IPOs in the US were SPACs. Since 2003, nearly 150 SPACs have raised more than US$ 17 billion. Over 60 SPACs under registration have a combined value of more than US$ 12 billion. SPACs have traded on Amex, OTC, AIM and even Euronext Amsterdam. SPAC sizes have ranged from as small as US$7.9m to as large as US$ 900m. SPAC offerings have included regions such as China and India, in addition to the US and Europe. Industry offerings include media, financial services, energy, shipping, consumer products, consumer finance, education, health care etc.

SPACs raise money faster than private equity funds, with greater liquidity, better clarity of investment objectives and rights of refusal (with substantial return of contribution) offered to the shareholders. SPAC public offerings are governed by SEC regulations and disclosure requirements. In May 2008, the SEC approved NYSE's proposed rule changes that aim to allow NYSE to list SPACs. While the NYSE specifies a minimum size, a SPAC is not required to have a prior operating history. Financial institutions in the GCC have the following alternative business opportunities with SPACs, namely, develop a SPAC based fund, participate in the development of a Middle East focused SPAC, and distribution of SPACs to expert investors. SPACs capture the art of managing risk without (minimal) risk.

Sporty Travel Times

The London Olympics have some interesting sidelines, such as missiles on rooftops, traffic congestion, immigration delays, food poisoning, and misplaced baggage, hours to get to the Games village, shortage of security personnel, ATMs running out of cash and gangs of pick pockets. The UK Treasury has abandoned its weekly gilt auctions for the period July 19 to August 16. A majority of bond traders are expected to be either 'working from home' or not at all during this period. The largest banks that are allowed to purchase securities directly from the Debt Management Office are along the main Olympic site transport routes. The Bank of England's plans to purchase gilts are also shelved since no new securities will be issued during this period. A leading newspaper sourcing news unethically, riots by the under privileged, members of Parliament padding their expense statements, bankers fixing lending rates – the UK has in recent times, a surfeit of embarrassments worthy of under developed banana republics.

Companies such as McDonald's and Coca-Cola have provided the International Olympic Committee with sponsorship funding of over $950 million in the four years up to the London Olympics. Financial demands have embarrassingly triumphed over cherished health values. Until zero calorie drinks and healthy menus become the norm, it appears that the London Olympics is the official sponsor of global obesity. Greed is good, fat is better is clearly the business logic, health considerations apart.

The UK generally, prayed for a Brit Wimbledon champion. Bookmakers, however, were relieved that Federer won. A Murray win would have resulted in over £5 million in payouts by bookmakers. Oxfam collected over £100,000 as a result of Federer's win. Nick Newlife bet £1,520 in 2003 at odds of 66/1 that Federer would eventually win seven or more Wimbledon titles. This piece of outstanding foresight and the bet was bequeathed to Oxfam by the late Newlife.

Samsung recently won a legal battle with Apple in the UK. The peculiar grounds of the ruling flummoxed both Samsung and Apple. Apple had tried to block the sale of Samsung tablets in the UK, claiming that three models of the Galaxy Tab resembled its own designs. Judge Colin Birss ruled, however, that differences in thickness and designs were noticeable, that Samsung devices did not have the extreme simplicity of Apple products and are 'not as cool'. If Apple appeals, they will be refuting the grounds that Samsung devices are not as cool. For Samsung, it is a bitter sweet victory. They can market their tablets in the UK but are now publicly recognized as not as well designed as Apple products.

One of Chris Guillebeau's favorite letters begins with 'Dear Boss, I'm writing to let you know that your services are no longer required'. 34 year old Chris believes that anybody can start a business with $100.

Chris has been living on the go since the age of 24 and has so far been to 185 countries. He has made money with publishing, travel writing, coffee trading and his best-selling book 'The $100 Startup', making money while doing things he likes intensely. Chris encourages people not to spend too much time building business plans and to use skills they already have. He is a self-professed travel hacker, using frequent flyer miles and deals to get around the world. Chris encourages people to focus on their personal point of convergence – what they like doing and what others are willing to pay for. He has never 'worked' in the traditional sense since the age of 24.

A Shanghai Lamborghini has given the phrase 'Shanghai-ied' a whole new meaning. Fake Lamborghinis are available in Shanghai for just around $ 35,000. Demand is strong, and the reservation period with a fifty percent down payment is as much as five months.

Sunny Side Up

The acronym 'HQ' is universally understood to represent 'Head Quarters'. The recent pursuit of the Happiness Quotient has now overtaken the very need for a 'head quarters'. Bhutan, a country with fewer than a million people, nestling between India and China, has rewritten the rules of macroeconomics. It is the only country to adopt Gross National Happiness ('GNH'), instead of GNP as the measure of welfare and development.

Under the constitution of Bhutan, government programs are required to be judged by the conditions for happiness that are generated. Bhutan has adopted an intricate model of four pillars, nine domains and seventy two indicators of happiness. The model focuses on factors such as, the environment, psychological well-being, health, frequencies of prayer and meditation, feelings of selfishness and calm, generosity, compassion frustration, education, culture, time use etc.

Mathematical formulas have been devised and are used as measures of the GNH index. Bhutan's GNH forms the basis of its planning process and the model recognizes that it is the State's responsibility to create conditions and an environment that will promote the happiness of its citizens. The basis of the philosophy of GNH is that the well-being of people does not depend upon Gross National Product.

The real measure of prosperity is the feeling of happiness, contentment and more importantly, the ability to share such feelings. A promise kept, a helping hand, compassion are valued aspects of society. The World Happiness Survey has discovered that some of the poorest countries have the highest levels of happiness. Businesses that are customer and employee centric are more likely to deliver long term sustainable results.

The Human Development Index ('HDI') is another useful measure of well-being and the standard of living in various countries. The HDI takes into account factors such as, life expectancy, literacy, child welfare and education. The objective was to shift focus from national income accounting to truly people centric policies. Access to knowledge is another key factor that in input to the HDI.

Norway has the highest HDI in the world, in all but two of the ten years from 2001 to 2010. Norway is one of the largest exporters of oil and gas, and maintains a welfare model with universal health care, and greatly subsidized higher education. The Norse mythological hero Thor (associated with hammer wielding, thunder, the protection of mankind, the day of the week Thursday etc.) has however, bestowed upon Norway, an energy resource with far greater potential to bring happiness to the country. Norway has large deposits of Thorium, a radio-active chemical element. Thorium has several advantages over uranium as a nuclear fuel, mainly that it is difficult to retrieve weapons grade material from a thorium reactor (incidentally also the reason why developed countries have studiously ignored thorium as a fuel). Thorium based reactors are likely to provide around 30% of the energy requirements of major developing countries by 2050 – a happy fuel indeed, 3 to 4 times more abundantly available than uranium.

Internet companies that contribute so much toward social networking and the spread of happiness are once again re writing the rules of valuation. From 'eyeballs' and 'mindshare', the new valuation metrics are ACSOI (pronounced ack-soy) and OIBDA. Adjusted Consolidated Segment Operating Income is a measure of operating profit and performance that places reduced emphasis on large marketing expenses. OIBDA – Operating Income before Depreciation and Amortization is another non standard accounting and valuation metric. Profits are reported after stripping out steep marketing and development costs. Lynn E. Turner, the former SEC chief accountant, referred to the spectrum of new accounting metrics as EBBS – Earnings before the Bad Stuff - more interesting than the good old EBIT measure.

Sustainable Food C(h)ain

Joel Salatin has a farm, some would say, better than Old McDonald's farm. The Polyface farm is a leader in the sustainable food movement and a symbol of an alternative food security system. Salatin raises grass fed cattle and beyond-organic chicken without an ounce of fertilizer. He is a farmer – philosopher who wants neither corporations nor government on his farm. His sustainable food system proposes decentralization of the food system, with fast food chains and big business organic food corporations, out of the way. The Polyface farm covers 550 acres and all products are sold fresh and locally with no shipments. The farm uses a unique system of mobile fences and portable chicken coops to move cattle and chickens to various sections of the pasture. The mixed use pasture utilization keeps the land in renewable condition and minimizes waste.

Only around one percent of Americans today earn a living through farming and not more than 10 percent is spent on food, whereas much more that amount is spent on healthcare. In a global economy where over 30 percent of all produce is wasted and over a billion people face hunger, Salatin's alternative food system holds the promise of a solution. The beyond-organic methods, that Salatin uses also need more labour and therefore, helps with local employment too. An estimated 108 billion people have lived on the earth since forever and around 7% of all humans ever born are alive today. Food shortage is not the reality, distribution and access is.

America's top 25 environment friendly companies include IBM, Hewlett-Packard, Dell, Accenture, Intel, Office Depot, Johnson & Johnson and others. In a 20 year period IBM saved over 5.4 billion kilowatt hours of electricity, HP has reduced its greenhouse gas emissions by 40 percent in the past 6 years, Johnson & Johnson uses solar panels to supply nearly 70 percent of its power at its Titusville production facility and more than 85 percent of Intel's energy comes from renewable sources. The world's top 10 includes two Indian tech companies and also BT for the world's largest wind power project by a non energy company. Office Depot now saves more than 3,000 tons of wood each year and provides customers with the knowledge to make trade-offs between financial and environmental considerations in their own buying processes.

The Republican presidential campaign in the US features Herman Cain. For a multitude of reasons, Cain has stirred up the otherwise dreary, grinding process, and has turned the game around. The former pizza mogul has never held elected office before and pushes that as a plus, as the real thing, not a politician. The Hermantor (as he likes to call himself), is a survivor of colon cancer, has studied missile technology, turned around a group of 400 Burger King units and later led the Godfather's Pizza chain. To Cain, creating jobs is as simple as delivering pepperoni pies. He summarizes himself as an 'ABC' (American black conservative) and in his most effective put down of president Obama, described him as a 'decent man' – the unsaid implication of incompetence was clear. His campaign pushes the 'Cain is Able' theme and his plan to introduce a first time value added tax in the US, and a uniform 9 percent tax rate has thrown the rules of Keynesian economics into the shredder and put on the table his own brand of 'Cainesian' economics. Herman punches powerfully way above his weight in debates, and just as the Vatican's curia had their second successive non Italian pope in over 400 years, white house staffers are preparing for the USA's second successive black American president, with a plan for change, this time hopefully for the better.

Taxing Doo – Wop Times

'Get a Job' was a number one song on the Billboard charts in 1958. The doo-wop song recorded by The Silhouettes was written by Richard Lewis after his mother urged him to get work. Getting a job today, however, is easier sung than done. Unemployment rates in developed countries continue to be in excess of 9 percent overall and higher than 15 percent among youth. Jobs of over 300,000 producers and workers in the poultry supply chain in the US are under pressure as a result of Chinese anti dumping duties. Sino-US ties bear an increasingly hen pecked and harassed look. USA's exports to China, in that category, have fallen by over 90 percent since October 2010. China's anti dumping duties range from 50.3 percent to over 105 percent. The fall in poultry exports has affected employment in the sector in the US. The Chinese have a marked fondness for dumpling and an equally marked distaste for dumping.

The US President has proposed higher taxes on the rich, now popularly known as the Buffet taxes. Warren Buffet surprised people weeks earlier by disclosing that on his annual income of USD 46 million, the tax rate was 17.7 percent, whereas a secretary in his company, with an annual income of USD 60,000 was liable to a tax rate of 30 percent. Buffet has also been urging the rich around the world to give more to philanthropic causes. However, the US Internal Revenue Service (IRS) has revoked over 70 tax exemptions, after discovering that tax benefits for philanthropy were being misused. Tax payers were found to be 'donating' assets to private foundations, availing tax deductions, while retaining control over the assets, to make payments to themselves or family members. In some instances barely 3% of the money benefitted charity.

California is the 'Golden State' in the US, with however, the worst credit rating of all States and a high 12 percent unemployment rate. California also has an estimated 2.5 million illegal immigrants. The State is faced with a growing shortage of tax-paying youngsters. Californians have proposed legislation that will give financial assistance to illegal immigrants who qualify as students under the program. Educating the young is a priority in an effort to sustain long term prosperity. This is California's own version of the Dream Act (a legislative proposal pushed recently in the US Senate). The Dream Act (Development, Relief and Education for Alien Minors) proposes to provide permanent residency to qualifying students, who graduate from US high schools. The intense search for law abiding, long term tax-paying residents continues.

US states are also proposing to help fix deficits and raise funds by privatizing prisons. Florida, Ohio and Arizona are leading the race to introduce privately operated or owned prisons. The US has a prison population of nearly 2 million and it costs an average of over USD 20,000 a year to maintain an inmate. Private companies have rushed in with speculative prison building projects with the expected result – a 'prison bubble'. Incarceration rates have not provided enough prison population to support these projects. A classic chicken and egg situation if ever there was one. Prison keeping cannot make money if the State needs the young out there, earning and paying taxes.

A software start-up company in Illinois has developed artificial intelligence (AI) that mimics human reasoning. The software works with data such as financial reports, sales numbers and sports statistics to write articles and news briefs. Hammond and Birnbaum, co-directors of the Intelligent Information Laboratory, set up Narrative Science and have taken AI coding one step further. Looks like AI is getting closer to Schwarzenegger's Terminator days and 'Getting a Job' for journalists will be much more difficult.

The Annihilators' Froth

Coca Cola is returning to Myanmar, after nearly sixty years. For Myanmar, it is a symbol of rejoining the world economy, a symbol of legitimacy, a symbol of capitalism and democracy, a flag and red carpet for foreign investments. Boxing, corn flakes, wrestling mania, cookies and popcorn will march in the wake of Coke. Coca Cola heralded the opening up of the Indian economy to foreign investments in 1991. The Cola and Star Trek go where no democrat has gone before. For The Coca – Cola Company of Atlanta, Georgia (originally, Coke was intended as a patent medicine in the late 1880's), the entry into Myanmar is not very good medicine for investors in the stock. The world's most valuable brand faces stagnation, as there are but two remaining markets left to conquer, namely, North Korea and Cuba. There is hope for Cuba yet, as the Cuban leaders have recently taken to using Twitter, and Coke cannot be far behind.

China has tried, for the past three decades to be recognized as a legitimate superpower. China has gone about acquiring systematically all the marks of a global superpower. Shanghai is flashier than New York, has more billionaires, and soon will have almost as many KFC and McDonald stores. In another decade, China's GDP will surpass the USA, in two decades China will even have more obese persons per thousand than the USA. China is now in the process of acquiring the capability to maintain its own deep sea aircraft carrier fleet and its very own space station. Following the path of global economic superpowers, China held its own Olympics and duly amassed an impressive tally of gold medals. None of this, however, helped China to be recognized as a legitimate economic powerhouse and doubts continued about the sustainability of China's economic success story. Wang Guowei has now solved the problem. The president of the state backed film production fund is financing a movie called The Annihilator. China, in 2014, will have the ultimate, legitimate symbol of global supremacy. Its very own super hero, 'The Annihilator' is a comic book style crusader against crime. A super hero that will compete in the market with Batman, Superman, Spider Man, Terminator, Iron Man and of course Captain America. China, with its impressive low cost manufacturing capabilities, could turn out super hero models in the billions, faster than any company in the USA. What China lacks is a supersized evil threat, befitting of a super hero, however, given Chinese enterprise, that cannot be far behind.

Meanwhile, the amazing banks of the USA continue their bold march toward destruction of capitalism. Basel III rules have left US banks short on capital and long on expected losses from defaults. In yet another, tricky piece of financial juggling, US banks are putting together structures that will enable them to take into account the value of intangible assets of borrowers (no doubt facing a shortfall of tangible assets). The structures involve banks paying insurance companies a fee for agreeing to purchase the borrower's intellectual property for a fixed price in the event of a default. This fixed price would then be reduced from the value of expected losses and counted toward the loan's security. Insurance companies are now the new pathway to providing capital to banks, also making it easier for banks to lend to technology, biotechnology, and start-up companies which generally value their ideas more than tangible assets. The International Centre for Financial Regulation has warned that 'such structures could prove problematic' – a massive understatement on the lines of a Greenspan-speak. The next big bubble would make the tragedy of credit default swaps look paltry, and is already blowing its froth. The banking industry plans to graduate from over valuing assets to valuing non assets.

The Fourth Leg

Tin Nyo delivers 'performance art' in New York. The audience gathers around, sipping cocktails while, on a concrete floor a skilled butcher skilfully dismembers a carcass. The performance called The Fourth Leg attempts to bring people closer to the origins of their food. Food that is usually packed, cut, filleted, frozen, in cubes or even nuggets is cracked, chopped and sliced fresh, skilfully, in the presence of the appreciative audience. Clearly this is an audience who would not understand what the noise at Occupy Wall Street was all about. Although very different, both approaches strive to bring people closer to their origins. Meanwhile, shoppers in the UK throw away over USD 20 billion of food, every year. The average British shopper throws away nearly ten percent of food bought and a significant number throw away nearly 25 percent of the food they buy. Similar data, although not available for shoppers in the US, is unlikely to be very different. The irony of the matter is that the problem of hunger in Africa could largely be solved if food wastage at homes in two developed countries is reduced.

Jean Paul Getty once said 'Money is like manure. You have to spread it around or it smells'. Companies in the US and EU are sitting on mountains of cash. Companies in the US with at least USD five million in cash or cash equivalents, hold over USD 1,600 billion in liquid assets. Apple has an estimated USD 80 billion in cash equivalents and marketable securities. Berkshire Hathaway has over USD 30 billion in cash and IBM generated over USD 80 billion cash (Buffet has now acquired over 5 percent of IBM) between 2005 and

2010, only marginally increasing its asset base during that period, using the cash primarily for shareholder buy backs and dividends. Investing in capital expenditure would lead to developments in infrastructure, productivity gains and more employment. This would improve the finances of households, companies and governments. Some economists have suggested that governments start taxing companies that hold excessively large amounts of idle cash and reward companies that spend or invest.

Recently in Cayman, a court determined that independent directors were guilty of wilful neglect of their duties and were asked to cough up over USD 100 million in damages. Company directors, now increasingly run the risk of being held responsible for wrong doing and even for simple neglect. Financial reforms have led to an increase in threats of litigation from shareholders and creditors. Previously, considered an extravagance, directors' and officer's (D&O) insurance policies that cover defence costs and potentially damages, are now poised for high growth in the current financial climate. New laws (for example the Dodd-Frank financial reforms in the US) give shareholders and creditors greater rights to pursue their claims with individual directors. Some insurance products protect asset managers from personal liability in the event that their funds collapse. A new insurance product called 'Darcstar' (Directors All Risk Cover) provides unusually wide risk coverage and, unless a risk is specifically excluded, it is covered. The Darcstar policy is just eight pages in length in place of the conventional twenty to thirty pages and more.

Meerut is an Indian city that is known traditionally for the uprising in 1857, sports goods, textiles and jewellery, has recently become well known in an unusual sector. Firms in Meerut have supplied ancient arms, ammunition, furniture and household items with exacting detail, for period movies and television serials. The breakthrough orders were for the movies Gladiator, 300 and the television series Spartacus. A growing number of movie producers now source medieval arms and costumes from Meerut. Indeed, a very different kind of performance art and fourth leg.

Top Guns

Today, employers' need of the hour is blunt honesty from their employees. Jurgen Schrempp (former CEO of DaimlerChrysler) once remarked that company subordinates let loose the truth only after 10 in the evening. With the current business environment, employers may be tempted to have personnel come in only after 10. An inventory of various sectors in 2011 revealed unusual growth sectors. A recent survey showed that retail shrinkage losses (essentially theft) have grown by nearly 7 percent in 2011. Over one thousand large retailers in forty three countries shared data that revealed that global retail shrinkage is now at USD 200 billion. Costs of loss prevention and security measures by large retailers was over USD 28 billion (up by nearly 6 percent). The highest retail shrink categories were accessories, outer wear, fresh meat, cheese, shaving products, perfumes and fragrances. Countries with the highest retail shrinkage rates were Russia, India and Morocco, whereas Japan, Taiwan and Hong Kong had the lowest rates.

Other big spurting increases in 2011 were the number of reported hacking incidents (RHIs) and gaming revenues. RHIs rose by over 37 percent and over nearly 300 million records were exposed or outright stolen in nearly 800 separate RHIs. Macao's revenues from gaming rose by over 40 percent in 2011. This is only a slight slowdown in Macao, over 2010 (a 58 percent growth). Macao's gaming revenues were nearly six times higher than Las Vegas. Even the slower growth forecast for Macao for 2012 is over fifteen percent. Bentley's sales in 2011 grew by nearly 30 percent over 2010. The new Ghost at Rolls-Royce also posted record sales in 2011. Bentley and Rolls were supported by Volkswagen and BMW, in their efforts to develop new models. In line with its growing popularity in China, Rolls-Royce rolled out a 2012 Phantom as their Year of the Dragon Collection with dragon like design features.

In 2011, Americans bought nearly 35 million Christmas trees, spending over USD 3 billion. Over 8 million trees made in China were sold in the USA, and it certainly looks as if America needs Chinese help even to celebrate Christmas and the New Year. Nearly sixty percent of American pet owners gave away holiday presents to their pets, spending roughly USD 5 billion on holiday gifts for pets during 2011. Over a third of Americans with pets hang Christmas stockings for their pets, and holiday gifts include toys, food, new bedding, clothing and grooming products.

Trafigura is a Geneva based company owned by employees. Trafigura is the world's second largest metals trader and a top three oil trader. The trading house's net profits recently crossed the one billion dollar mark. This represented an over 60 percent increase over 2010. Factors contributing to the exceptional profits were prolonged volatility in commodity markets, caused by social upheaval, natural catastrophes. Base metals traded by Trafigura were up by over 25 percent and overall revenues surged by over fifty percent in 2011.

Bjarke Ingels is a Danish architect who feels strongly that waste is an unexploited resource and the key is to finding out what it is good for and how to feed it back into city metabolisms. Ingels' design of a waste management centre combines a giant incinerator with a ski slope. Waste will be converted into energy to heat up homes, while at the same time providing the city with a ski resort. The incinerator will also playfully produce a super smoke ring with each ton of carbon dioxide released – improvements in technology will lead to smaller and fewer smoke rings. The technology of waste incineration and power generation has been in the pipeline since the 1950s and has now matured into an efficient technology.

Wheels of Business

'Make it Easy on Yourself' is a popular song that was a hit for Jerry Butler in 1962 and a number one hit for the Walker Brothers in the UK. Concerned investors are probably hoping fervently that politicians in the EU and USA will make it easy on them. It really not as difficult as it may seem to make it easy. There are those who would suggest that the USA's economic troubles could easily be solved by taxing the millionaires club a bit more. Warren Buffet was the latest to complain about low taxes on the rich. New York's tax rate on incomes exceeding US$ 500,000 is less than 9 percent, California's top tax rate for millionaires is less than 11 percent, Maryland and Connecticut have top tax rates on high incomes of less than 7 percent. Rationalization of tax rates and military spending could pay down USA's debt by over USD 2 trillion over the next 7 years.

However, the million dollar snag is that nearly 45 percent of those in Congress are themselves millionaires and the rich representatives are going to stiffly resist any increases in their own taxes – so their solution is to cut government support spending on the poorer sections of society. As Buffet and others have pointed out, the rich earn a significant portion of their income from long term capital gains and dividends, and the tax rates on these have been severely cut over the years. Over the past 25 years the wealth of the richest 1% of Americans has risen by over 250 percent. The 18th century Chinese emperor sought a peaceful eventual retirement and built a Palace of Tranquil

Longevity to meditate and write poetry in a corner of the Forbidden City. Qianlong, who was in fact a contemporary of George Washington, had realized that there are limits to the utility of vast wealth and power. Buffet would have been delighted with the Emperor's private paradise.

In Copenhagen, over 35 percent of commuters get to work on bikes. High fuel prices, congestion and pollution have seen cities turning to a cleaner and greener urban commuting alternative that also provides excellent exercise as a collateral benefit. Cities such as New York, Mexico and Santiago have added miles of biking lanes. Jens Skibsted's company Biomega produces designer bikes. Biomega makes bikes that fold, glow in the dark (safety and convenience features), and bikes that have frames made from bamboo or frames that use aerospace aluminium bonding methods. Biomega partnered with Puma to make high fashion bikes and sales have grown in recent years at nearly 30 percent a year.

According to the World Bank, the rate of bankruptcy among Indian firms is four in ten thousand (0.04 percent). The corresponding historical rate in the USA is close to 4 percent or an astonishing 100 times higher. The Howrah Mills Company of Kolkata is still spinning yarn since the 19th century, some hotels in Japan date back to the 8th century, a few German breweries were set up in the 11th century and at least one Italian bank dates back to the 15th century. In stark contrast, IBM stands lonely on its 100th birthday. Of the current top corporations, only Apple and Amazon are likely to make it to that landmark. Economists do not expect companies such as HP, Dell, Cisco, even Microsoft and Oracle to be endowed with such longevity. Business firms that have stood the test of time are based on values and ideas – not on specific product groups or technology. Making it easy to use, easy to buy, easy to access will help corporations last the distance (Jerry Butler's hit is still popular 50 years on).

Windows Sesame

Microsoft is finally taking window cleaners very seriously. In a response to a spree of applications being built for the iPhone and iPad, Microsoft's Windows division has begun to overhaul its Windows platform with touch screen interface features, newer ways for Windows to be compatible with devices such as tablets, and access to easy- to - use lightweight applications through an online store. As in real life, the cat and mouse game with touch screen applications is likely to see the end of the mouse.

Mr. Ma is the ma-n behind 'Alibaba', the e commerce trade platform and shopping search engine. For good measure, the group has also registered the name 'Alimama'. The Alibaba that almost everybody knows was a kind person who helped his village. It is however, almost 'Close Sesame' for Yahoo, thanks to Alibaba. Ma has expressed his interest in buying Yahoo Inc. Alibaba is now valued at over USD 30 billion. Yahoo and Alibaba are linked through a 40 percent equity stake that Yahoo holds, that Ma has attempted t buy back. Foreign ownership however, complicates entry into sensitive business sectors in both American and Chinese markets. Chinese ownership of Yahoo could lead to major privacy risks and concerns relating to Chinese access to data relating to millions of Americans and business units. Data centric cloud computing can bring in heavy weather. Meanwhile the number of internet users in China has topped 500 million. That is twice as many as in the USA (245 million), and more than the EU population, while India, Japan, Brazil and Germany, each have between 75 million and 100 million users.

As financial markets readjust and rebuild, collateral management is now a core area for market participants. Collateral is intended to provide security against credit risk and default. Collateral management involves monitoring and where necessary valuing collateral right through the life cycle of the transaction and of the collateral itself. Third party custody and management of collateral, where feasible, is also an increasingly favoured arrangement. Better collateral management can result in better management of risks and lower funding costs.

Albert Einstein was wrong after all and Capt. James T Kirk and Mr. Spock of the USS Enterprise (Star Trek) were right – there is a particle faster than light. Scientists at the Cern nuclear research centre have proven that some subatomic particles do travel at a speed greater than the speed of light. Investors could use this to get back in time to a place where the Euro did not exist, currencies and banks were sound and debt was not measured in trillions. Star Trek's star travellers used 'warp drive', with the technical breakthrough achieved in the saga around the year 2063. The Star Trek series was the first to assume the possibilities of such speeds and their vision of a breakthrough in 2063 does not sound so fanciful after all.

Some things, however, don't and won't change. The Pentagon's annual budget of over USD 700 billion, included over USD 47 million on cookie dough (nearly 16,000 tons), over 5,000 cases of lip balm and more than USD 1 million over the past three years on caprines used in training ('caprines' is their scientific name for goats). Purchases also included classic statues, bean bag toys, sun screen, fish tags for tracking salmon and trout and, actors who perform role playing (portraying friendly and not so friendly locals). Expectedly, none of these are likely to be on a list of budget cuts. Likewise, 47 years later, Taco flavoured Doritos are still around. Arch West who discovered the crunchy triangular Doritos in the 1960s during a family vacation in Mexico, was recently laid to rest at the age of 97.

Wutburger

The German Language Society's chosen words of the year for 2010 were 'Wutburger' – enraged citizen and 'alternativlos' – no alternative. Sadly, these words seem most appropriate now, in view of the current economic plight of the USA and several European countries. Over 20% of the world's economically active youth between the ages of 15 and 24 are either outright unemployed or severely under employed. In the USA, unemployed youth are known as 'boomerang kids'(back home after college), in Spain – 'mileuristas' (earning no more than 1,000 Euros a month), in the UK – 'neets' (not in education, employment or training), in Japan – 'freeters' (freelance workers), in North Africa – 'hittistes' (those who lean against the wall), in China – 'ant tribe' (college graduates crowding into flats or basements in big cities). The world seems full of indignant, unemployed youth, some of whom have not had a job in two years. Three examples of non conventional occupations gaining ground are – 'ethical hackers' who work to guarantee the security of networks, 'fantasy brokers' – who make dreams come true e.g. a clerk wants to be a stand-up comedian for a night, and 'food historians' – cook in the style of any decade and study the social history of food.

The Big Mac Index (BMI) developed by The Economist, now includes India (in July 2011 for the first time). The BMI uses the product price to indicate the real rate of exchange between two currencies. The recent BMI shows that the Indian rupee and the Chinese Yuan are undervalued vis-a-vis the US dollar by 53 percent and 44 percent respectively. This reality was reflected in the 46 percent surge in Indian exports from April to June 2011. The BMI, introduced in 1986 gave rise to the term 'burgernomics'. The informal indicators of purchasing power and the rate of exchange appear to be closer to reality than the formal exchange rate. A comparison with the prices of a common service (the Big Mac is a product with material and labour variables) yielded similar results, using the average cost of a male hair cut - the Hair Cut Index.

As a result of years of trade surpluses, China is in the enviable position of holding foreign exchange reserves amounting to nearly US$ 3 trillion. The vast scale of these reserves could, on paper, mean that China could purchase all taxable real estate in Manhattan and Washington D.C. (estimated at US$ 520 billion), all of the outstanding debt of Spain. Portugal, Ireland and Greece, all the equity of Apple, Microsoft, IBM and Google (estimated at less than US$ 1 trillion) or all of the farmland in the US (around US$ 1.9 trillion). While key economic sectors flounder in the US, defence/ military spending accounts for over 20 percent of the US federal budget, and the US military spending amounts to over 42 percent of the world's total (China comes in at 7 percent).

The economics of sports in the US are also undergoing a change, for practical reasons rather than financial reasons. Research, based on trauma related incidents between 1980 to 2009 (30 years data) has shown that the most lethal impact sports in the US are football, track and field and baseball, with boxing coming in at a distant fourth place. The results, covering research into over 22 impact sports, is likely to affect parental interest, student interest, degree of school oversight and the Big A (advertising). Clearly, it is much safer to be a food historian, ethical hacker or fantasy broker, than a sportsperson. Another safer, brainy and sporty business idea from Lumos Labs is a 'brain gym' that has tailored game plans (brain pushups), designed to strengthen memory, attention and decision making.

X Men and Moonshots

John Steinbeck famously remarked that ideas are like rabbits. The principle is that one starts out with a couple, nourishes them and in a relatively short span of time there are dozens of ideas bouncing around. Google recently sponsored 'Solve for X' – a conference where innovators, scientists and businessmen were encouraged to propose radical technological solutions to the biggest global challenges. Google calls the process encouraging 'moonshot thinking' to develop breakthrough technologies and develop solutions beyond the imagination and parameters of the everyday business world. The purpose of Solve for X is the create a pipeline of world changing ideas focused initially on energy, climate change and health – issues that politicians and businesses are known to walk away from. These issues, however real, are largely side stepped since solutions in these areas involve 3X thinking (three generations ahead). Technologies for water desalination, bio fuels, elevator towers that stretch to the moon were some areas discussed.

'Meet and Seat' is a KLM program that permits passengers to upload their profiles from Facebook and Linkedin. These profiles can then be used to choose 'acceptable' seatmates. Other airlines including Air France, Lufthansa and Virgin Atlantic have also attempted to introduce profile sharing and social networks among their frequent fliers. Malaysia Airlines has introduced 'Mi-iBuddy' that allows ticket holders to check if any of their 'friends' are either on the same flight or at their destination on the days they are travelling in. 'Friends' can select seats together. The Danish start-up plainly allows users to submit itineraries, view profiles of other travellers and connect with travellers on the same routes. Satisfy, out of Hong Kong, allows users to submit flight moods (e.g. talk shop, chat casually, sleep off), languages spoken and more specific preferences about seatmates. KLM passengers with confirmed reservations are given seat maps for the flight showing seats of others who have shared their profiles. While 'social seating' trends are increasing, some airlines (Air New Zealand, Air-Asia X in Malaysia and Vueling of Spain) let (not so social) passengers reserve empty seats beside them for a fee.

Reliance Entertainment is an Indian media and entertainment, production and distribution company. In addition to producing Indian 'Bollywood' movies, Reliance has been involved with popular movies such as The Help, Real Steel, Cowboys & Aliens, and more recently War Horse. Meanwhile, DreamWorks Animation is looking at a joint venture with state owned Chinese media groups. Shanghai is likely to get its own state of the art production studio. Flat box office takings in the US are prompting Hollywood producers to take a serious look at movies for the Chinese market. China adds three new screens a day (the Chinese box office market grew 30 percent in 2011) and will be the world's biggest cinema market within a few years.. Shrek and Kung Fu Panda would probably look more realistic if made in China. The Chinese media tycoon Bruno Wu is reviewing opportunities to acquire

Hollywood film companies, and Summit Entertainment (Twilight), Lions Gate and Miramax have been reported as initial prospects. Culture, censorship and commercial sense represent the triangulation of drivers for the Chinese entertainment industry. And no, Brian Wu is not an exponent of Kung Fu.

Amazon has launched a a shopping website in India, appropriately (somewhat) called Junglee.com. In line with government regulations, the website will only redirect shoppers to sites of retailers and will not sell products directly. The shopping portal will allow shoppers to compare prices and features online. Over 14,000 brands offering at least 12 million products will be offered. The portal could be an amazing game changer for Amazon especially since the call (contact) centres can be located in India with no complaints from either US trade and online shoppers will be comfortable with Indian accents.

Xiang Feng

China has invested massive sums of money in developing a homemade regional jet. The mid-size (90 seats), short haul aircraft was named the Flying Phoenix (Xiang Cheng) by popular vote from nearly 400,000 internet users. China hopes that its indigenous aircraft will one day provide competition for Airbus and Boeing at least in the home market.

India, on the other hand has pursued a very different, and economically more efficient policy of managing the transportation issue. India and China, each clock an estimated 5 billion passenger fares each year (excluding commuting within 50 kms.). This years' weather conditions lock down in China during the holiday season highlighted the magnitude of the problem. One of the most amazing management successes and startling recoveries in recent times has been that of the Indian Railways. India has had business school graduates and economists as Ministers. However, the Indian Railways was turned around, not by a management graduate, but by a politician from arguably one of the country's poorest states. Five years back the Indian Railways was written down as a lost cause. Energetic and focused attention, together with speedy decision making shorn of bureaucratic stalling has swung this train around in its tracks. The Indian Railways now has an annual surplus of over US$ 3.5 billion and cash surplus of over US$ 20 billion.

Better asset utilization, quicker deployment of freight trains, investment in rolling stock, improved productivity at the manufacturing locations, resulted in cash profits and enabled reduction in freight rates and passenger fares. An organization that employs over 1.5 million personnel (the world's largest utility employer), sent senior staff to premium management institutes in India, the US, France and Singapore. E tickets and booking by SMS were introduced. The Indian Railways competed round for round with the flashy private sector airlines as well as the low cost carriers, and has come up ahead.

The Indian Railways transports nearly 17 million passengers and 2 million tons of freight each day. The Indian Railways has both the longest and busiest suburban rail systems in the world and operates from nearly 7,000 stations. The world's longest railway station (over 1,000 metres), the Lifeline Express (a hospital on wheels), the longest rail run (2,340 miles), the Palace on Wheels, and the oldest running locomotive in the world are other outstanding features of the over 150 years' history of this Government of India enterprise. With aviation fuel touching new highs, this Xiang Feng is once again up and flying.

Two unique enterprises in India's commercial capital are food related. Mumbai has a system of hand delivered lunch time meals ('*dabbawala*') all over the city, in colour coded aluminium boxes. This system employs zero technology and does not employ a single college graduate. Over 200,000 meals are delivered each day in Mumbai with six sigma error rates. The system has been studied by business schools and corporations such as Coca-Cola and Daimler. Team work and time management result in annual revenues estimated at between US$ 20 million to US 35 million. The other huge success story is that of a simple popular low cost Mumbai breakfast snack ('wada pav'). The wada pav clocks an annual turnover in Mumbai of over US$ 20m. Its not just the sales, in both cases, the direct costs are less than 10 percent of sales values!!

China would probably, do well to revisit its Xiang Feng plans and look to innovative, low cost solutions. The GCC could also hugely benefit from a rail system that can be run as a profit centre and truly network nationals of all member States.

Yours, Mine and Our s

Everybody, every bank and investment company and every country has their very own Green Monkey. The Green Monkey is a colt that was sold as a two year old for $16 million, a world record auction price. The colt was so named after the owner's connections with The Green Monkey golf course in Barbados (the island has green monkeys) and the colt was also foaled in the Chinese year of the green monkey. The Green Monkey, raced only thrice, was retired after only a year, did not win a single race and showed no inclination to run competitively. The cerebral occupations of the 19th and 20th century were mathematician and scientist in that order. The 21st century is likely to have 'Chaostician' (pronounced 'kay-oh-tician') as the key occupation, as delivering results in times of strategic chaos becomes increasingly important in the business world.

'Yours, mine and ours' (a 1968 movie starring Henry Fonda and Lucille Ball and remade in 2005) gets a whole new 21st century meaning. Africa is a continent with mineral wealth that has not yet been fully mapped, explored or estimated. South Africa alone has mineral wealth estimated at nearly $3 trillion. Ghan (gold), Nigeria (oil), South Sudan (oil), Libya (oil), Zambia (copper), Guinea (bauxite), Botswana, Zimbabwe and Namibia are other examples. As both Western governments and China make a beeline for African mineral deposits, governments in Africa seek to increase state intervention (regulation and taxes) on the mining sector to raise revenue quickly. In addition to taxes, miners are likely to be increasingly asked to dish out local goodies such as roads, railways, schools, hospitals and investments in power plants and refineries. Divestment regulations will also make it mandatory in some instances to sell equity stakes to locals.

Working well into the golden years appears to be crushingly good economics. The previous broadsides that people should retire earlier to free up jobs for the younger generation, have slowly sunk. However, historical data in both developed and developing economies has shown that high employment rates among the older workforce is invariably accompanied by high rates among the younger workforce as well. People working, at any age, earn money and spend that money, this in turn creates jobs for the younger generations in an expanding economy. People retiring early place a burden of pension and taxes on the younger generations, while reducing average disposable incomes. Early retirement ages reduce wage bills but result in ballooning pension costs. No society can be prosperous and progress if it eventually pays an increasing number of people not to work (retirement benefits). Working long hours and working long years are here to stay. Here today and gone tomorrow is no longer good economics. In fact econometrics shows that if the retirement age was brought down to 40, most young people would be employer, however, average per capita incomes would reduce, taxes would increase, demand would reduce. Retirement, economically speaking, is moving from a practice to a concept.

The 18th century English rhyme, 'Sing a Song of Sixpence' included the lyrics 'pocket full of rye, four and twenty blackbirds, baked in a pie, when the pie was opened the birds began to sing'. More recently, private equity fees of 'two and twenty' have come under increasing criticism. Private equity managers charge a 2 percent management fee and a 20 percent share of profits. The sharp edge of the pie is that the 2 percent management fee is calculated on capital committed, not on capital invested. The management fee could amount to as much as 20 percent of invested capital. Academics at Yale have shown that private equity fund managers are (not surprisingly) better at enriching themselves than their investors. In times of economic crises, two and twenty is plenty.

Zeitgeist

Zeitgeist (attributed to German philosopher Hegel) refers to the spirit of the time, the intellectual fashion prevailing, the dominant school of thought that influences the culture of any period. Hegel believed in the influence of the social construct or the environment in which people lived. This theory contradicted the 19th century Great Man theory (Scottish writer Thomas Carlyle) which stated that history is a result of the actions of geniuses and heroes. Business ideas of the 20th century and the 21st century are a combination of Zeitgeist and the Great Man theory.

Sir Tim Berners-Lee (Sir Tim) invented the World Wide Web in 1989. Computer networking is not recognized as a traditional science and that is the only reason Sir Tim was never awarded a Nobel Prize. His greatest contribution was not charging for his idea, and making it absolutely free without even a royalty charge. Kim Ung-Yong is a Korean civil engineer known for his contributions in the field of hydraulics. Kim (born 1963) is on record as the most intelligent human ever. At age four, Kim was solving complex mathematical problems on television and was fluent in English and German. Kim started university courses as a child, completed a doctorate in physics and joined NASA at age 12. Canadian JD Millar's simple, yet brilliant solution of painting a white line down the middle of roads, in 1930, dramatically reduced the rate of automobile accidents. Two 20th century brilliant business ideas are the 1972 concept of Lonely Planet travel guides, and the 1959 doll idea of Ruth 'Barbie' Handler. More recently, a 13 year old British school boy invented the Smart Bell – a doorbell that rings the person's mobile phone when not at home. Dr. Martin ('Marty') Cooper's idea of portable handsets in the 1980s changed the face of communications technology. Before Marty, communications were based on point to point calls. Marty believed that people should call people not places, and invented the portable handset. His original prototype weighed around a kilo and his early vision was to bring down its size to fit the palm. Fittingly the first mobile call in 1973, by Marty, from Sixth Avenue, was to Bell laboratories. The rest as they say is history, Blackberry and now Steve Jobs. A humble pensioner Annie Bell Adams is credited with the first class-action lawsuit, claiming that big banks fixed LIBOR and made adjustable rate mortgage repayments more expensive. 'Brave-heart' Annie's lawsuit takes on traders at 12 of the biggest banks in Europe and North America.

Celebrity Net Worth recently published a list of the 25 richest people of all time, with numbers adjusted for inflation. The 14th century African King Mansa Musa I topped the list with a net worth of USD 400 billion. Mir Osman Ali Khan is the richest Indian of all time with an estimated net worth at today's values of USD 230 billion. Carlos Slim was ranked at 22, and Warren Buffet barely managed to get into the list, last at number 25. Mir Osman Ali Khan (the last Nizam of Hyderabad who passed away in 1967 at the age of 80) used the famous Jacob diamond (now worth USD 95 million) as a paperweight. The richest American of all time is John

Rockefeller with an estimated inflation adjusted net worth of USD 340 billion.

Red Bull recently sponsored Felix Baumgartner to leap from over 128,000 feet, at faster than the speed of sound, watched by over 8 million people. The fastest free fall ever by a sportsman, however, has been recorded by cyclist Lance Armstrong who has been dropped by Nike, RadioShack and others after substance misuse allegations. Armstrong and Tiger Woods were the brand 'untouchables' of the Nike brand. Armstrong beat Tiger's brand freefall record by weeks.

Zombie Investments

A large number of private equity fund investors have funds in non performing funds with fund managers who have no opportunity of achieving investment returns that would earn them a performance bonus. However, the structure of the funds permits them to continue to earn a management fee based on the size of the portfolio. Fund managers therefore hold on to the investment portfolio and 'earn' the management fee. All the while, the value of the portfolio continuously declines and the management fee does not even encourage 'caretaker' maintenance activity to protect the investments. These 'zombie' funds are navigationally 'dead in the water' and are rapidly moving from caretaker status to undertaker status.

Stock market regulators in China are clamping down on 'pump and dump' operations by investment companies. Guangdong Zhonghngxin (Gee Zhee) was accused of racking up profits of over €50 million by inflating market prices of stocks. Gee Zhee set up television programmes, advertising programmes and analysts reports to encourage investments in specific stocks. Insider trading and skewed financial reports have long been considered par for the course. While the rest of the world moves to a common base of IFRS (International Financial Reporting Standards), Chinese equity investments appear to be mired in its own brand of IFRS (Inherently Fraudulent Recommendations on Stocks).

Chinese merchants are struggling to collect their money from smaller daily deal websites (DDWs) in Chiina. There are over 4,000 Groupon clones in China, selling everything from clothing and, cosmetics to entertainment. In 2011 Chinese DDWs raised over $500 million as venture capital, lured by quick cash returns. This October, however, only 16 new DDWs opened in China, whereas 1,017 ceased operations. The larger Chinese DDWs, such as Gaopeng, Lashou, Wototuan, Manzou and Sohu are spending on aggressive marketing programs and expanding their sales teams in an effort to sustain transaction values. This has made the effective costs of customer acquisition much higher for smaller DDWs. Coupon sites in China, it would appear have very rapidly graduated from achieving critical mass to a state of critical mess (and default).

Yum! (Kentucky Fried Chicken, Taco Bell, Pizza Hut etc.) has more than 4,000 stores in China and plans to take this number to 9,000 by 2020. The company set up nearly 300 stores up to September this year and owns more than eighty percent of its stores in China. A new store in China costs around $500,000 to set up and could return $300,000 each year for the next five years without major refit capital expenditure. To finance this expansion of owned stores China, Yum! is franchising out company owned stores in the US and in the UK. The spectrum of the Pizza Hut menu is being broadened to include various day part meal segments, giving a whole new meaning in the UK to 'lundinner' – as the brand tries to pull in more of the office going footfall (more like tummy fall in this case) that often combines a skipped lunch with an early dinner in a casual dining environment.

The 'LINHUS' (List of Intangible Heritage In Need of Urgent Safeguarding) of the UNESCO, includes some interesting heritage practices. Among these are the Yaokwa, the Naqqali and the Limbe. The Yaokwa is a Brazilian ritual for maintaining social and cosmic order – probably most useful to politicians and economists in the EU. Naqqali is the art of dramatic story telling in Iran – international nuclear watchdogs have by now deeply studied Naqqali. Limbe (Mongolian folk songs) involves a calming technique of circular breathing – of great benefit to the chairpersons of central banks. Then, there is the Koredugaw, a rite of wisdom performed by in Mali – of great benefit to all modern day politicians.

Zugzwang

'Zugzwang' is a term from chess that describes a situation where one in compelled to make a move which one would prefer to avoid. The 21st century business Zugzwang is likely to be a contra – compulsion not to make a move, when one would prefer to make a move.

The USA is sore with India on a number of counts. Not the least being that students of Indian origin regularly bag the Spelling Bee contest top spots and, since 2007 an Indian has claimed the world chess championship (the US formerly holding the distinction of dethroning the former Soviet bloc champions). Now, it seems that, adding insult to injury, India is likely to be the world's largest exporter of buffalo meat. This sort of turns on its head and even gives a whole new twist to the legendary Buffalo Bill, the Wild West adventures and Red Indians. Given time, these are likely to become adventures of the not so wild east and not so red, Indians. India will be the leading exporter of beef in 2012, ahead of even Australia and Brazil. India's exports of buffalo meat have tripled since 2009 and are now over 1.525 million tons a year. Global demand for beef is forecast to rise sharply due to demand from South Asia and the Middle East. Outsourcing of water buffalo is something America cannot complain about, unlike the call centre (or BPO) operations in India. The west certainly cannot have its beef, eat it and complain about it too.

About the Author

Savio is a financial advisor with a background in economics. Savio has completed his chartered accountancy, certified public accounting and certified internal auditor examinations. He is a graduate in Commerce & Economics from the Bombay University and an alumnus of St. Stanislaus. Savio also has a Masters' in Economics and a Doctorate in Strategic Studies. He has worked in the finance field on projects in over 27 cities in India, and in Armenia, UK, Australia, USA, Kuwait, Iraq, Iran, Saudi Arabia, Bahrain and Kenya. Savio lives in Kuwait with his wife Mallika (also a finance professional) and advises a diversified family managed group. Savio is also an FIDE registered and rated chess player. He participated in the World Seniors Chess Championships in Aqui Terme, Italy in 2015.